GW00600852

Think Tanks
and Problem Solving

Think Tanks
and Problem Solving

Paul I. Slee Smith

BUSINESS BOOKS LIMITED

LONDON

First published 1971

ISBN 0 220 66894 9

This book has been set in 11 pt. Baskerville and printed at the Pitman Press, Bath for the publishers, Business Books Limited registered office: 180 Fleet Street, London, E.C.4 publishing offices: Mercury House, Waterloo Road, London, S.E.1

MADE AND PRINTED IN GREAT BRITAIN

CONTENTS

PREFACE

So much has been written and talked about 'Think Tanks', sometimes referred to as 'Brain Factories' or 'Brain Banks' and less picturesquely as independent research institutes, mostly of American origin, that it is interesting to enquire into their origins and role in society: to look at the different kinds of think tanks, advisory corporations like the powerful Rand Corporation in Californi adeeply involved in policy research for the US Air Force: philosophical think tanks such as the Centre For The Study of Democratic Institutions concerned with great crisis issues facing the world today: industrial think tanks like TEMPO specialising in business strategies: hard science institutions such as Battelle Memorial who combine the physical sciences with techno-economic studies and futurist institutes like the Institute for the Future who take a long, critical look at the year 2000. Although differing in structure, disciplines and methods, each of these organisations—intellectual watch towers—is qualified to do the advanced thinking and analysis so essential in order to understand the many faceted problems crying out to be resolved.

No matter how difficult these may be, how unpredictable the future, the best hope of finding answers to fit the questions lies with the intellectual elite of the think tanks—the cadres of scholars, scientists engineers and other experts who are able to mobilise all the resources of the hard and soft sciences and to develop new methodologies and novel approaches to problem solving.

This may be an admission of failure on the part of government, management and labour, but the chaotic state of the world today—the drifting from one crisis to another; the total inadequacy of attempts to solve the highly complex problems of the Jumbo Jet Age with the kind of approach used at the time of Langley, Wright and Blériot—all this tends to undermine the

confidence we have in our decision makers whether in government or industry. There is a growing realisation that with
major problem solving as it affects society the emphasis tends to
be all wrong: solutions are sought before problems are understood and with the new, instant solutions new problems, some
of greater magnitude than the old ones, crowd in to embarrass
and harass the policy makers. There is also a general unwillingness to question the boundaries of problems before
trying to solve them and insufficient attention is paid to the
need to build up a broad basic data base so as to be able to
answer the many vital questions relative to the problem. In
other words, modern problem solving, whether it touches
affairs of state or commerce, calls for the professional touch;
experience is not nearly enough. Indeed, the only promising
new approach seems to lie with the think tanks, whose staff
of several disciplines are trained to study problems and to
analyse the situations confronting them before attempting to
prescribe possible solutions. Accelerating technological change
and lagging social progress are creating crisis situations in
many areas, particularly in the social field, so that an entirely
new approach to problem solving is long overdue.

This book sets out to tell the story of the think tanks and
what they are trying to achieve. They are not miracle makers,
but in their orderly scientifically based efforts to present
acceptable alternative solutions to some of the complex problems vexing society they can at least offer the prospect of
reducing the degree of uncertainty and/or risk in taking long
term policy decisions.

Human knowledge and human power meet in one; for where the cause is not known the effect cannot be produced. Nature to be commanded must be obeyed; and that which in contemplation is as the cause is in operation as the rule. FRANCIS BACON

From the Latin *Novum Organum* Aphorism III

INTRODUCTION

The knowledge industry sets out to make available for the first time the orderly and logical use of man's vast intellectual resources, mobilising for this task the special skills of scholars and scientists, utilising all the varied tools of science and fashioning new methodologies and techniques.

By mixing pyschology with mathematics (to form what Professor Isaac Asimov calls psycho-history) the knowledge industry predicts the future, taking medium and long range forecasting out of the realm of crystal ball gazing. While there is no absolute certainty about these predictions, the new mathematical equations of the futurologists give a high degree of probability to many of the forecasts so that planning can be carried out in the light of expected events.

Faced with the growing complexities of totally new environments man looks at the future—troubled and perplexed. Although the new technologies have brought him unprecedented material prosperity, greater knowledge, greater leisure, emancipation from old shackling beliefs and a longer life span, they have also brought him the prospect of total annihilation with nuclear weapons, gross pollution of the environment and, largely through automation, a deadly monotony of life.

It would seem that the new technologies are controlling man's destiny instead of man controlling them; the engine appears to be running away with the driver! This is because many of the really complex problems are never properly understood before attempts are made to solve them, and then they are tackled piecemeal or on a hit-or-miss basis. There is no effort made to analyse the situations that confront those in authority, to know more about their causes and dimensions. The knowledge industry offers man an opportunity to do this, and not only to predict his future but to control his environments and not leave the future to chance. But everything depends on those at the controls on their ability to create the right kind of future!

What is certain is that the conventional institutions we have grown up with are incapable of meeting the many and varied challenges which modern civilisation is constantly throwing up. Their inadequacy stems from many causes but none more important than the fact that too much reliance is placed on experience; too often the planners look to the past for guidance rather than trying to peer into the future. What is basically wrong with the governmental machine is that it was designed for an age that has long past; it lacks the flexibility and adaptability which modern problems demand. Moreover, the conditions are not right for advanced thinking and the right people have not been recruited to carry out the expert analysis of critical future environments and interactions which the long range planners so badly need if sound decisions are to be made. What is needed is the kind of deliberating super-intelligence found only in organisations such as think tanks of the calibre of the Rand Corporation. These seem to be the only institutions in sight with the knowledge potential to manage man's future. One recalls Malvina Reynolds folksy song:

> '*Oh, The Rand Corporation is the boon of the world;*
> *They think all day long for a fee.*
> *They sit and play games about going up in flames:*
> *For counters they use you and me, Honey Bee,*
> *For counters they use you and me.*'

Think tanks are important because there is no other institution to do their kind of job. So much more knowledge is needed today that no government department nor even the biggest industries are big enough to have any longer all the experts in everything. It has been estimated that the US Government does not take a single major decision in national security without first taking advice from outside agencies such as think tanks like TEMPO, the Rand Corporation and university-attached institutes under Government contract.

Decision makers in government, however, do not expect think tanks to provide them with clear cut answers to complex questions or to make up their mind for them, but to set in front of them sets of alternatives and background information and data which they can use as guidelines in arriving at 'best possible' solutions to problems.

Government Departments are under constant pressure from a number of sources to attain various goals: to build so many houses; reduce crime by a certain percentage; lower the birth-rate; improve the health service, etc., and the eyes of officials are therefore closely focused on the goals. Think tanks, while fully conscious of the importance of the goals which have to be reached, are more interested in the process by which it may be possible to attain them and they stress the urgent need to re-examine and, if necessary, to re-define the goals in the light of any new facts which come to light as the problem is studied. With a fast chang-ing environment all systems, if they are to function properly, must be able to accommodate constant changes within the living social organism. It is largely because think tanks are sensitive to change, and have the flexibility to adapt their thinking to the new conditions imposed by technological developments, that they offer man the best chance of intelligent planning for the future. The 1968 Delos Declaration, in some ways a rather odd document, makes this significant point:

> 'Linear planning must be replaced by systems of feedback. For planning for, we must substitute planning with. For goals which bind the present, we must substitute processes which generate a continually self-renewing future.'

But think tanks not only give advice to governments, they help to solve some of the acute problems affecting society and also assist industry in strategic business studies, problem solving and innovations. In areas of great uncertainty, no matter whether it concerns the planning of urban developments, health services, police, welfare, pollution or the planning of research and develop-ment in a company, think tanks are able to bring to the problem new skills and new methodologies, and to apply the same sys-tematic research attention to domestic and industrial studies as to space probes and the design of nuclear weapons. One of the fields of study particularly applicable to industry is the transfer of technology and in America think tanks have been particularly active in exploiting the inventions, discoveries, innovations and developments produced as a direct result of the nation's massive R & D programmes in defence, space and atomic energy.

What is not always appreciated is that the germs of great discoveries sometimes lie forgotten and unrecognised in the experiments and demonstrations which scientists carry out in what may seem unrelated fields. As far back as 1785 the English chemist, Henry Cavendish first demonstrated to his friends at the Royal Society the odd fact that when electric sparks were passed through air a change took place resulting (as we understand it now) in the combination of oxygen and nitrogen and leaving behind eventually a residue of some gas that could not be sparked into any union. These first fumbling experiments laid the foundation for two major discoveries centuries later; the synthesis of nitrates from the air and the isolation of the rare gas argon.

The recognition and eventual utilisation of potentially valuable discoveries and innovations is an important function of some of the hard science think tanks, such as the Denver Research Institute which has been a pioneer in the technology transfer field. It acts on behalf of NASA in analysing and evaluating the use made by industry of the technological spin-off from America's vast space programme. Since this recovery project started in 1967 great interest has been shown in it and during the first year over 23,000 requests for technical reports were identified and analysed.

From what has been said so far it might appear as if think tanks operate only in the rarefied atmosphere of government departments and the corridors of power in very big business, but this is not so. The methods of approach to problems, the special techniques so successful in areas of defence, social security and economics, are often directly applicable to all sides of industry and commerce. The knowledge industry is all the time paying out big dividends in the form of new techniques and these are freely available to be exploited in solving present day problems and peering ahead towards solutions of future problems.

Such broad based techniques as systems analysis, cost analysis, theory of games and the basic Delphi procedure are legacies of the think tanks, so too are the many highly specialised methods of commercial forecasting, some of which, such as the input–output technique, are being extensively used in industry for forecasting the changes in demand caused by changes in end markets or by technological changes in design of a product. Input–output which is a very simplified model of the economy that traces the flow of goods and services between industries is likely to be widely adopted by all progressive companies in North America within the next two years. This novel method, developed by Samson Science Corporation, one of the really progressive commercial think tanks, provides a listing of products, materials, parts and labour required to manufacture a specific product, and gives a framework for a detailed analysis of a product's sales to its end markets, including the government, consumer and export sectors of the economy.

While the think tank as we know it today is an all American invention the idea of recruiting a multi-disciplinary team to do forward planning is not particularly novel. Shortly after the Second World War several large companies on both sides of the Atlantic toyed with the idea of grouping together a few of their more brilliant and speculatively minded scientists and scholars and setting them the task of just thinking about company problems. It was hoped that by the cross fertilisation of ideas the company would reap a rich harvest of profitable suggestions. In practice, the operating costs of the experiment proved difficult to justify in terms of actual money-making brainwaves, managements became impatient for results but neither the whip nor the carrot succeeded and most of the groups were gradually disbanded. Perhaps failure was inevitable; too much was expected too soon, and without the proper structuring of problems little real progress was likely to be made. However, in one or two cases the think group idea really did work very well. Fifteen years ago the EMI company had a highly successful multi-disciplinary 'Forward Thinking Group' to look into business computer developments. On the applications side, in 1956 there was very little historical experience on large scale computer needs and applications and the EMI think tank was given the task of thinking about all the various aspects of the business and factors most likely to affect future growth; to try and forecast what the market wanted; what the costs and benefits would be in various situations; what government policy was likely to be in relevant areas; and what changes in technology would be possible and economically viable and by when.

One of the people who was much concerned with computer developments in EMI in 1956, Mr K. M. Simpson (now with PA Management Consultants Ltd.) gives as his opinion that the EMI Forward Thinking Group was an enlightened attempt to combine a think tank with an engineering development project to ensure that the technical developments converged with the commercial, political and other developments.

ACKNOWLEDGEMENTS

The author is grateful to the following research organisations who have supplied him with information about their activities on which this book is based:

SYSTEM DEVELOPMENT CORPORATION, 2500 Colorado Avenue, Santa Monica, California, USA

HOUSTON RESEARCH INC., 6001 Gulf Freeway, Houston, Texas, USA

GENERAL ELECTRIC COMPANY, 816 State Street, Santa Barbara, California, USA

BOOZ-ALLEN APPLIED RESEARCH INC., 135 South La Salle Street, Chicago, USA

PLANNING RESEARCH CORPORATION, 1100 Glendon Avenue, Los Angeles, California, USA

IIT RESEARCH INSTITUTE, 10 West 35th Street, Chicago, USA

STANFORD RESEARCH INSTITUTE, Menlo Park, California, USA

IR AND T INTERNATIONAL RESEARCH AND TECHNOLOGY CORP., 1225 Connecticut Avenue, NW, Washington DC, USA

THE HOOVER INSTITUTION OF WAR, REVOLUTION AND PEACE, Stanford University, Stanford, California, USA

RESEARCH TRIANGLE INSTITUTE, Research Triangle Park, North Carolina, USA

INSTITUTE FOR THE FUTURE, Riverview Center, Middletown, Connecticut, USA

TRW SYSTEMS GROUP OF TRW INC., One Space Park, Redondo Beach, California, USA

CAMBRIDGE CONSULTANTS LTD., St. Ives, Cambridge, England

SOUTHWEST RESEARCH INSTITUTE, 8500 Culebra Road, San Antonio, Texas, USA

INSTITUTE FOR DEFENSE ANALYSES, 400 Army-Navy Drive, Arlington, Virginia, USA

THE BROOKINGS INSTITUTION, 1775 Massachusetts Avenue, NW, Washington DC, USA

SPINDLETOP RESEARCH INSTITUTE, Ironworks Road, Lexington, Kentucky, USA

PROGRAM ON TECHNOLOGY AND SCIENCE, Harvard University, 61 Kirkland Street, Cambridge, Massachusetts, USA

THE CENTER FOR STRATEGIC AND INTERNATIONAL STUDIES, Georgetown University, 810 Eighteenth Street, NW, Washington DC, USA

THE FRANKLIN INSTITUTE RESEARCH LABORATORIES, The Benjamin Franklin Parkway, Philadelphia, Pennsylvania, USA

YALE UNIVERSITY, New Haven, Connecticut, USA

HUDSON INSTITUTE, Quaker Ridge Road, Croton-on-Hudson, NY, USA

RESOURCES FOR THE FUTURE INC., 1755 Massachusetts Avenue, NW, Washington DC, USA

MINISTRY OF TECHNOLOGY, Dean Bradley House, Horseferry Road, London, SW1

MIDWEST RESEARCH INSTITUTE, 425 Yolker Boulevard, Kansas City, Missouri, USA

CENTER FOR RESEARCH ON CONFLICT RESOLUTION, The University of Michigan, Ann Arbor, Michigan, USA

THE ROCKEFELLER FOUNDATION, 111 West 50th Street, New York, USA

BATTELLE MEMORIAL INSTITUTE, 1755 Massachusetts Avenue, NW, Washington DC, USA

THE INSTITUTE FOR ADVANCED STUDY, Princeton, New Jersey, USA

ARTHUR D. LITTLE INC., Acorn Park, Cambridge, Massachusetts, USA

THE RAND CORPORATION, 1700 Main Street, Santa Monica, California, USA

THE CENTER FOR THE STUDY OF DEMOCRATIC INSTITUTIONS, Santa Barbara, California, USA

QUANTUM SCIENCE CORPORATION, 245 Park Avenue, New York, NY, USA

DENVER RESEARCH INSTITUTE, University Park, Denver, Colorado, USA

FOREIGN POLICY RESEARCH INSTITUTE, University of Pennsylvania, 2508 Market Street, Philadelphia, Penn., USA

CARNEGIE-MELLON UNIVERSITY, Mellon Institute, 4400 Fifth Avenue, Pittsburgh, Pennsylvania, USA

THE MASSACHUSETTS INSTITUTE OF TECHNOLOGY, Massachusetts, USA

P.A. MANAGEMENTS CONSULTANTS LTD, 2 Albert Gate, Knightsbridge, London, SW1

I   WHAT ARE THINK TANKS?

Derivation

The term 'think tank' is a piece of American slang whose origin is unknown although 'think box' has long been identified with 'the head'. The 1908 edition of Partridge's *Dictionary of Slang and Unconventional English* uses 'think tank' in the sense that it was the brain of the individual, generally implying it to be crazy. That is, a person referred to his head or brain in the sense: was his 'think tank' still working? In the *Dictionary of American Slang* (Harold Wentworth and Stuart Berg Flexner) 'think tank' is held to be synonymous with 'think box' and brain. The present sophisticated meaning for the term does not appear to have been given until the early sixties. William Safire in his book *The New Language of Politics* (1968) says that by 1964 the meaning had developed to its present usage—a group of advisors for developing ideas, plans and the like.

The first editorial reference to 'think tanks' which the author can find appears to have been in *Time Magazine* (5 August 1966); the *New York Times* Magazine Section mentioned the phrase again in 1967 (16 April, pp. 28ff) and from then onwards it was taken up by a number of publications. However, the current use of the term was already well established at that time, and, as William Safire points out, by 1965 it was fashionable to refer to the non-profit research and advisory corporations in America as 'think tanks'.

The think tank is really the brainchild of Dr Vannevar Bush when he was at the Massachusetts Institute of Technology. He had a theory that given the right conditions of work, organised intelligence from civilian sources could outproduce the military in creative ideas, and he pointed to the success of the Radiation Laboratory at MIT during the Second World War to prove his point. It was Dr Bush who was largely instrumental in persuading

General H. H. Arnold of the US Army Air Corps that the only way to break really new ground in weapon design was to recruit the best academic brains available and to give them a free hand. Fortunately for the US Air Force, General Arnold was sufficiently imaginative to like and act on the idea. The result was the formation of Project Rand later to become the famous Rand Corporation.

In the United States today there is a tendency to narrow down the term 'think tank' and to imply a research organisation, like the Rand Corporation or the Hudson Institute, not involved in the mainstream of business. However, the interpretation which the author prefers is somewhat broader than this and takes in many of the contract research institutes as well as the non-profit advisory and some profit-making advisory corporations; indeed, organisations deeply involved in the knowledge business but not actually generating any hardware as the direct result of their work. As Julius Duscha (*Saturday Review*, 23 September, 1967) aptly describes think tanks: 'Their common aim is to try and strip away the fat from the conventional wisdom and lay bare a sinew of facts and ideas. They are supposed to be the reducing salons of the intellectual world.'

Mr Joseph R. Feldmeier, Vice President and Director of The Franklin Institute, says that think tanks are characterised by:

1 Serving a single sponsor such as one of the military services.
2 Staffed by people from a broad spectrum of scientific disciplines, branches of engineering, social sciences, economics, etc.
3 Their problems tend to be very complex in nature and are therefore attacked as a team effort with representatives from the various fields of learning mentioned above. Study reports from the think tanks generally end up giving a set of options from which a decision can be drawn.

The operations of a think tank embrace a multitude of concepts, techniques and approaches which have one aim in common: reduction of the degree of uncertainty and/or risk in taking long term policy decisions by:

1 Defining the fundamental factors influencing the decision.
2 Assessing the present and future significance of those factors.
3 Thinking through and evaluating the consequences of various courses of action in the light of those factors.

The cynic might, perhaps, be forgiven for thinking that some of the long range forecasts produced by think tanks or tank thinkers look so far ahead that their perpetrators will be well beyond earthly criticism by the time their chickens come home to roost. However, most people concerned with the work of think tanks would agree that their methods of approach to problems is valuable, in terms of today's problems as well as tomorrow's. The key ingredients are:

1 Staff of several disciplines training their minds on the problem.
2 Emphasis on creative solutions.
3 Deliberate questioning of the boundaries of the problem.
4 Experience and technique in structuring the problem and controlling the group assigned to it.

The name 'think tank' although expressive is somewhat misleading as it tends to give the impression that whatever 'thinking' is done is in isolation in some kind of monastic cell cut off from outside contacts of influences, rather like goldfish in a glass bowl. Most of the organisations referred to in this book do not work in isolation; research is inter-disciplinary, all manner of different kinds of scholars and scientists, engineers and technologists taking part, the aim being to combine the insights of the hard sciences and the behavioural sciences. Informality is the keynote of most studies, the approach to a problem varying with each kind of situation. In those think tanks where attention is focused on complex problems in areas of great uncertainty, several different types of intellectual tool may be used to stimulate ideas, to open up new fields of enquiry, for example games, simulation, seminars, conferences, questionnaires and some unusual brainstorming techniques. No matter how problems are tackled it is almost certain that a great mass of information and data will have to be processed and analysed and for this work computer facilities are made available. In think tanks specialising in the hard sciences, such as Battelle Memorial Institute and IITRI Institute, experimental work is carried out in conventional laboratories and workshops, although here the new management technologies play an increasingly important part. Even in those think tanks devoted to philosophical studies, the impact of technology and electronics (particularly computers and communications) has been considerable. By making computers serve as extra brains the think tanks have greatly enlarged their scope and capacity as problem solvers.

Criticism of Think Tanks

Think tanks are looked upon with growing suspicion by an increasing number of people, many of whom see something sinister in the influence they have on decision makers and policy planners in government.

Probably the most valid criticism of the think tank is that it is an exotic flower that flourishes best in the unhealthy atmosphere created by vast government expenditures on defence and aerospace research and that it shrivels up and dies in the cold air of highly competitive commerce and industry. However, it is as well to point out that big government spending programmes are never so tightly budgeted that they do not allow a bit of slack and opportunities certainly exist for those engaged in research to put their feet up and engaged in free speculation about this and that, to formulate new problems and ask questions and it is often out of all this philosophy and speculation that new ideas are born. After all the young Isaac Newton was engaged in little more than daydreaming when he tried to solve the self-created pseudo-problem: 'Why do things fall?' And his thoughts reached far beyond the thought that the apple was drawn to the ground by gravity; how far did gravity reach, that was what puzzled Newton!

One of the reasons why the think tank idea has never really caught on in this country is because the British people are naturally suspicious of experts whereas in the United States the expert is venerated. However, there is reason to believe that this attitude is fast changing. The new technologies, the quickening pace of life, a rebellious youth and the shadow of conflict, all these are creating situations where help from outside sources may have to be sought if any progress is to be made in solving the complex problems facing our society.

Politicians resent the growing power of the small cadres of scholars and scientists whose advice is continually being sought by the executive: military leaders see in the think tanks a challenge to their authority. They may still have their finger on the trigger but the weapon is sighted by someone else; industry and commerce, long accustomed to being regarded as centres of research tend to resent the intruders.

Think tanks are necessarily detached, much of their work being classified and therefore secret. Even in the private sector the cloak of secrecy covers so much of their work and even future research has now become very hush hush, what is called 'factor S' (S for secrecy) weighing heavily with all futurologists. This air of mystery about think tanks, the publication of so many half truths about their functions and responsibilities has given them a bad press, while a great deal is made of the criticism that an intellectual elite is threatening the whole process of democratic government. Think tanks are said to be obsessed with nuclear war, to be too detached from ordinary everyday life and ordinary problems. However, the record of the think tanks, and particularly the advisory corporations, since the end of the Second World War has been an impressive one; although the peace has been an uneasy one the great powers are still at peace. True one twelfth of the world's annual output goes to the world war industry, but Armageddon still isn't here. The policy planners at Rand and similar institutions must surely be given some credit as it is on their analysis of situations that key decisions have been taken.

The First Think Tanks

The Rand Corporation is always considered to be the archetype of the American non-profit research and development organisation; indeed, the name Rand was coined from these terms (although one joker has said that it means 'Research and NO Development'). Project Rand was established by the US Air Force in 1947, being formed to help the generals with research on the broad subject of intercontinental warfare (other than surface). Its emergence as an advisory body to help the policy makers has always been hailed as a confession of failure on the part of the planners to grapple with their own problems, and this, of course, is true. Government agencies, most of them over-burdened with administrative details, can no longer be expected to understand fully the problems they are being asked to solve. Moreover, they have not the time to give to the fundamental thinking about great natural issues that is so necessary for long range planning. Help is needed to analyse complex situations, to collect, process and interpret the mass of information and data that flows into the various departments. Certainly it is true that Rand's success sparked off the establishment of several more think tanks by other government agencies, notably RAC by the US army, CNA for the Navy, IDA for the Joint Chiefs.

However, long before the emergence of Rand as a research and advisory corporation at the end of the Second World War, several independent research establishments (although at the time they could hardly be called think tanks) had already been in existence for a number of years. The Franklin Institute in Philadelphia was founded in 1824, 34 years after the death

of Benjamin Franklin, by a number of prominent Philadelphia citizens. It was called The Franklin Institute of The
State of Pennsylvania for The Promotion of The Mechanic
Arts and had for its aim the upgrading of technology and bringing
applied science to the solving of national problems. The Franklin
Institute set out to apply basic scientific principles and knowledge
to the solving of technical problems and to forsake the old trial
and error methods generally favoured by technologists of the
nineteenth century. For example in their first investigation—
into the causes of steam boiler explosions in steamboats—they
tackled the problem in a then novel way, combining theoretical
scientific knowledge with practical engineering experience. In the
early days of the Franklin Institute men with scientific knowledge
joined with practical men to provide know-how that would
otherwise have been lacking, and it was this bridging of science
and practical applications that was to be so successful. It speaks
well for the foresight and enthusiasm of those early pioneers that
what started as a local mechanics' institute should develop into a
scientific and technical association that was to win worldwide
acclaim. Out of the Franklin Institute grew the Franklin Research
Institute, founded in 1946, one of the first of the independent
research institutes to encourage inter-disciplinary research.

At a time when the Franklin Institute was already well established, and science and technology in America were beginning
to become rather sophisticated in looking for the professional
approach to research, Mr Griffin and Mr Little opened a small
chemical laboratory in Boston in 1886 offering 'inventors and
manufacturers every scientific help in developing new ideas'.
This set the pattern for the future—applied science and research
directed towards innovations and the improvement of industrial
processes and products. In the early days of ADL (as it is com-
monly known) the company showed great foresight and a good
deal of courage in introducing to American industry some
startling new ideas, later to develop into massive industries such
as artificial silk (Cross and Bevan's viscose) and cellulose acetate,
one of the early thermoplastics. Probably the most fundamental
change in the structure of ADL took place in 1938 when it
became technical consultant to the Chemical Fund, a Wall
Street investment trust devoted to investments in the stocks of
chemical and process industry companies and found it necessary
to penetrate deeply into business problems involving technology,
trying to answer the client's many questions about the world
outside his own country.

Today ADL, one of the largest profit-making contract research organisations in the world with a staff of more than 1500, devotes half of its staff and energies to applied research and engineering and half to management consulting. Whereas 50 years ago ADL was primarily concerned with the hard sciences, today the emphasis is on the soft sciences, many of the problems this think tank is being asked to solve having more in common with sociology than chemistry—market research, regional development, long range corporate planning. Probably the outstanding characteristic of Arthur D. Little Inc., is its ready adaptability to the new technological environments and ability to tackle any kind of problem, provided it is meaty enough to satisfy the scientists and scholars at headquarters. Projects range from cosmetics to nuclear weapons and space probes to studies of civil disorders.

The Mellon Institute dates back to 1911, first as a department of industrial research at the University of Pittsburg and later (1913) as The Mellon Institute of Industrial Research and School of Specific Industries, all this through the philanthropic efforts of the wealthy Mellon brothers whose aim was to develop a coupling of science and technology as an aid to industry. The Institute continued its activities as part of the University of Pittsburg until 1927 when it was incorporated as The Mellon Institute, a non-profit research establishment.

Throughout the distinguished history of the Mellon Institute, the emphasis has been on studies which contribute to man's understanding of his physical universe and solution of problems bearing on his health, welfare and comfort. However, Mellon is probably better remembered for the major contributions it made to the American chemical industry; work carried out at the Institute created new industries, such as the Visking Corporation, Plaskon Company Inc., and Dow Corning Corporation. In other cases, large new branches were added to existing companies, the most outstanding being the Chemicals Division (now Union Carbide Chemicals Company) of the Union Carbide Corporation. Altogether the Mellon Institute has been responsible for over 650 novel processes and products.

Battelle Memorial Institute at Columbus was found in 1923 as a memorial to the memory of Gordon Battelle, a North American industrialist 'for the encouragement of creative research—the making of discoveries and inventions—the better education of men—the discovery, licence and disposal of new technology.'

The Institute was established as a 'not for profit' corporation operated by a self-perpetuating Board of Trustees. Battelle's laboratories in Columbus, Ohio, opened in 1929 with a staff of 25. Today 6000 people are working for this think tank at major research centres in America, Germany and Switzerland. Research embraces many fields and at any given time upwards of some 600 projects are under way in the Columbus laboratories and many of these are in technical–economic fields: economists evaluating the computer as a decision making tool in freight-trucking operations; analyists studying the forces which shape the US and European economies and projecting economic profiles to 1975; machine dynamics research, materials research and hundreds of other projects in the hard sciences.

Another big research institute, IITRI, was founded in Chicago in 1936 as Armour Research Foundation of Illinois Institute of Technology, an independent not-for-profit contract research centre covering all the physical and biological sciences and their related technologies. From a handful of scientists who started IITRI 34 years ago, the present institution has grown to a very large research establishment with a worldwide reputation employing some 1800 and with an annual sales volume exceeding $28 million as against some $40 million for Battelle.

The general pattern of research carried out at IITRI is somewhat similar to that of Battelle, typical programmes ranging from basic investigations, through applied research and engineering, to new product development, particular emphasis being given to it. Every year IITRI ploughs back a significant percentage of its funds to support internal research and to provide its scientists and engineers with an opportunity to explore promising scientific concepts. Many of IITRI's internally sponsored research projects have been highly successful. For example, the development of techniques for modern magnetic recording at IITRI resulted in hundreds of patents licensed by manufacturers throughout the world. IITRI has syphoned its work on business management problems out of the mainstream of research and a profit-making company, Corplan Associates, was formed over ten years ago to cover such areas as market research, product evaluation, production systems, financial planning and organisation audits, all of which play a vital role in new product introduction.

Since the end of the Second World War a large number of independent research institutes, most of them not-for-profit, have come into existence to meet the urgent needs of American industry and to exploit the many wartime developments just waiting for large scale commercial application, e.g. jet propulsion, gas turbines, radar, antibiotics and nuclear energy. The time was ripe for a massive R & D effort; moreover, plenty of government money was available for defence projects and the wealthy foundations, such as Ford, were only too eager to endow worthwhile projects. Added to this, a new regional consciousness was springing up in many States of the Union of the need for bigger and better research facilities to supplement those made available by industry, Federal agencies and the universities. States who had no think tanks looked enviously at those who had them. The West, in particular, felt badly neglected when it looked across at the East with its many research institutes—the eleven Western States had fewer industrial research laboratories than the single State of Connecticut. Industrialists and business men were quick to appreciate that the not-for-profit research institute could be of great benefit to a community, contributing to its economic growth, stimulating industrial activity, encouraging the fuller uses of natural and human resources and helping to improve the image of the region as progressive and technologically oriented.

Moreover, State officials saw in these research organisations promising opportunities for pioneering corporate business activities, attracting new science based industries to the district and providing employment and also training facilities in the use of the new technologies. Some States even took an active part in helping to start up a potentially important research institute. Spindletop, a not-for-profit applied research centre formed in 1961 by a group of far-seeing industrialists, business men, Kentucky officials and educationalists was supported by the State Government which not only gave it a 130 acre site on which to build its laboratories, but in addition contributed generously towards its endowment. A chain of regional research centres, all of them not-for-profit, came into existence: Midwest, Southwest, Stanford, Gulf South, North Star, Spindletop, Research Triangle, etc. The largest of these, Stanford Research Institute, started as a one man organisation in 1946 and now has a staff of more than 3000 of whom half are professionals. Its work covers a wide spectrum of research interests—the physical, biological and social sciences, engineering and the mechanical arts—and even as early as 1948 the Institute embarked on a series of research programmes in the fields of industrial economics and management sciences. Research programmes in the hard and soft sciences have led Stanford to pioneer large scale interdisciplinary research projects (e.g. long range industrial planning and weapons systems analysis) that are unique in many ways. As early as 1958, Stanford started systematic work in the field of technological forecasting and for several years the Institute has offered a long range planning service (LRPS) as part of a package deal to companies and agencies.

One of the most important of the postwar think tanks is TEMPO, a unique long range planning and inter-disciplinary study organisation of the General Electric Company, one of the world's major industrial corporations. Since its founding in 1956, TEMPO has conducted under contract hundreds of advanced studies of a highly diversified nature for leaders of national and local governments and private corporations. By participating in the United States' most advanced technological projects, TEMPO has developed expertise in the development and applications of the total systems approach. Senior officials in government departments use TEMPO's findings as the basis for important decisions, while major organisations have supplemented the work of their own research departments with TEMPO's worldwide perspective and independent viewpoint.

Another very interesting think tank is Triangle Research which is part of a unique research complex. Created as the focal point of North Carolina's Research Triangle, this Institute is built in the centre of a 5000 acre park midway between the region's three major universities and adjacent to some eighteen industrial and government research organisations. While Triangle Research has very close university affiliations, it is also in touch with its non-university scientific neighbours, and discussion and consultation with their professional staff is encouraged.

Project Rand, the forerunner of the Rand Corporation, was set up in March 1946, by the American Air Force in an attempt to bring together civilian scientists and the military not only to develop new and better types of military hardware but to apply scientific and mathematical techniques to strategy, tactics and logistics. General Harp Arnold who conceived the idea of an advisory organisation for the Air Force was far sighted enough to realise that with the great advances made in science and technology, and particularly with the development of nuclear weapons, military planning had become so intricate that it needed the combined efforts of the best brains from civilian scientists and the military planners. At first Project Rand was organised as an adjunct of the Douglas Aircraft Company in Santa Monica, California, but in 1948 the organisation became the Rand Corporation independent of any private company. Although today it is still the Air Force's principal advisory organisation, it does a great deal of work for other Federal agencies and private sponsors. What is particularly interesting about Rand is that its outstanding success, particularly in the evolution of the systems analysis approach to problems (arising out of the earlier operations research techniques), lead directly or indirectly to the formation of a whole host of advisory corporations set up by the military in America to help with their planning. Some of these organisations were actually splinter groups of the parent Rand, e.g. the mighty System Development Corporation was formed originally as the System Development Division to help the US Air Force with its training programmes. The Rand Corporation has always been preoccupied with research on a broad strategic basis and when projects tend to narrow down and become specialised, for example over concern with tactical matters, devices, training, etc., if is felt that the time has perhaps come to form a new type of organisation with new terms of reference.

Another great difference between Rand and other advisory corporations is that it enjoys greater degrees of freedom. It is an integral part of the Corporation's policy that opportunities should be created for Rand staff to carry out research of their own choosing; its so-called '20 Percent Policy' means, in effect, that 20 per cent of a researcher's time is spent on keeping abreast of developments at the frontiers of knowledge. Created at a time when the United States Government was badly in need of advice of exceptionally high calibre, Rand did all, and indeed a great deal more, than was asked of it in the fields of missile and satellite technologies, helping the country to re-plan its entire defence system. However, apart from work directly concerned with security Rand has been responsible for introducing some startlingly new mathematical tools, the concept of system analysis and programme budgeting, apart from work more closely linked with the hard sciences, such as research on new structural materials, such as titanium and beryllium. As more than one writer has said to paraphrase Voltaire, if Rand did not exist it would be necessary to invent it.

Rand has been particularly successful in attracting the right kind of professional staff, may of whom have left to help build up other research organisations. For example, Dr Herman Kahn, author of *On Thermonuclear War*, was a Rand nuclear strategist who left to start up The Hudson Institute, a kind of smaller edition of Rand but one less closely tied to its military sponsors.

2 THINK TANKS AT WORK

Think Tanks or Think Factories

In the context of present day research activities, the term 'think factory' might be a more accurate description than 'think tank' as some American establishments have a payroll of factory dimensions: Battelle Memorial Institute has a staff of 5900 (2600 at Columbus, 2100 at Hanford, 800 at Frankfurt and 400 at Geneva): Stanford Research Institute 3112 (1407 professionals): IIT Research Institute employs 1854 (815 professionals): Southwest has 1175. A. Little Inc. (for-profit institute) has 1500. Another (for-profit) research institute Planning Research Corporation which specialises in systems analysis for industry, state and federal agencies has a staff of 3579 professional and support personnel. The professionals, half of whom have advanced degrees, represent 50 areas of knowledge in the physical, life and social sciences, mathematics, nearly all branches of engineering and economics. If TRW Systems Group qualifies as a 'think tank' as some people maintain, then this (for-profit) corporation has a payroll of 17,000 at 25 locations throughout the world. The powerful GEC's TEMPO employs a full time staff of 300 professionals which includes an extremely broad cross section of skills and experience.

The System Development Corporation employs rather more than 3000, two thirds being professional–technical with more than 10 years' experience. The mix of professional disciplines found at SDC is made up of data processing 40 per cent; human factors 17 per cent; operations research 7 per cent; engineering 5 per cent; other disciplines 21 per cent.

Rand has grown to 1100 employees, approximately half being professionals. However, bigness is not an essential qualification of a think tank, and at the other end of the scale there are many medium size and some very small establishments. Typical of the former is Midwest Research Institute with 350 researchers, technicians and their supporting staff. This organisation has won international recognition in many fields and particularly in the collection, organisation and dissemination of information in specific fields, for example, the Germanium Information Centre established at MRI for the world's major germanium producers.

Hudson Institute employs only 35 with a list of consultants running to over 100 and the International Research and Technology Corporation or IR & T less than 25 (with a number of consultants). The Institute for Advanced Study in Princeton, New Jersey, which is devoted to the encouragement, support and patronage of learning—of science in the old, broad undifferentiated sense of the world—has some 40 permanent members of which about 20 constitute the Faculty. Outside the United States the few think tanks that exist are quite small. For example, Germany's first think tank, the Holste Institute, started with a mere handful of specialists and a budget of 3 million marks in comparison with the Max Planck Institute in Munich which struggles along on a miserable million marks.

The State based research institutes in the USSR are somewhat similar to the British research stations run by Mintech and hardly qualify to be classed as think tanks and the sixty or so research establishments in Japan, although inter-disciplinary and organised in some respects on American lines lack the freedom and independence which characterise the American think tanks. If the name think tank is applied to the various look-out institutions concerned mainly with technological forecasting there are several in France, notably Centre International D'Études de Prospective in Paris, two in Sweden, and one in the Netherlands, Austria, United Kingdom and, of course, many in North America.

A very interesting policy making organisation in Athens which might well be called a think tank is known as the Delos symposium and its creator is the remarkable man, C. A. Doxiadis who runs a multi-million dollar ekistics or consultancy in the Greek capital. Ekistics is the new science of human settlements and Doxiadis' organisation sets out to study the social architecture of the human environment rather than its physical structure. Discussion on current problems facing civilisation is largely restricted to symposiums at which social scientists, biologists, lawyers, painters, architects and historians contribute.

There are also the modest 'study groups' or 'prognostic cells' functioning in certain European and Asian capitals which have rather different terms of reference to those working in the USA, although it might be correct to find a parallel in the Centre for the Study of Democratic Institutions where Fellows gather daily around the conference table to think and talk about the basic issues of the day. This think tank with its staff of 24 men (and one woman), writers, philosophers, scientists, social scientists and lawyers with two bishops and two ex-college presidents meet to talk about the problems facing twentieth century man.

The think tank label is being applied rather loosely to all kinds of strange bodies, some of which might possibly justify the term but others certainly do not. One of those that does justify the name is the unit set-up by P & O, the world's largest shipping group. This is made up of 40 graduate engineers and naval architects to exploit the inventions and ideas based on the suggestions sent in by P & O sea-going and shore staffs. Already it is claimed that some of these inventions enjoy great success and one, the Pilgrim Nut, an ingenious device for dismantling and holding propellers and tailshafts is in regular use in submarines, merchant ships and the *Queen Elizabeth 2*. Britain's new Post Office Corporation claims to have formed the first British think tank, a 10 man team with Lord Snow at its head and a budget of £15–20,000 to think about new ideas to improve the Post Office, and particularly its outdated telephone system.

The best claim which any British organisation seems to have to call itself a think tank is Cambridge Consultants, a small but thriving engineering research and development company which specialises in solving other people's problems. It has a staff of 50 made up mainly of chemical, mechanical and electronic engineers and a few physicists, their average age being about 28. Situated at St. Ives, only a short drive to Cambridge, the company has a close relationship with the University and quite frequently calls upon members of its staff to act as consultants on special projects.

The People Who Work in Think Tanks

While it is taken for granted that those who work in think tanks are well qualified academically in the various disciplines, they are not necessarily the most brilliant scholars and their IQ may not be oustandingly high. As Lord Snow points out, a lot of people with a high IQ appear to have nothing else but a high IQ. Think tank men are essentially people who, faced with a problem, first ask themselves the question 'Why should it be solved? rather than 'How can it be solved? and sometimes it is the answer to the first question that is the most pertinent and helpful in answering the second one, if, indeed, it has to be answered!

The solution to the kind of problem which so often faces the research institute seldom comes from the so-called logical approach made by those who seem best fitted to do the work, and research in one direction can sometimes yield surprising results in an entirely different and unrelated field. When Rand Scientists applied some of their advanced mathematical techniques to problems confronting cancer researchers at the Sloan-Kettering Institute an unexpected pay-off was a solution to a missile trajectory problem that had bothered them for some time.

Unlike researchers in industry those who work in think tanks are not essentially apparatus men and methodologists nor are they overmuch concerned with quantitative facts, except as essential background material, but in order to tackle the kind of assignments that come their way they are very much concerned with creative thinking, realising that the solution to the immediate problem may itself provide another that is even more difficult to solve than the original one.

Unlike the conventional research establishments which expect to have to deal with clear cut situations and well defined problems, think tanks are often expected to deal with uncertainties, issues where objectives may not be clearly defined, where considered judgements have to take over from proven facts and where it is not always possible to apply modern mathematical techniques and high speed computers to produce a neat solution. To meet the needs of such situations think tanks may have to design new tools capable of being used under conditions where the problem may not be completely understood, futures uncertain and aims little more than guesswork. This all sounds rather woolly, but think tanks like Rand & Hudson are expected to tackle projects that almost fall into the realm of science fiction, such as determining the character of the next generation of tactical weapons or judging the stability of the thermonuclear balance. As Bruce L. R. Smith points out in his book on *The Rand Corporation*, 'such esoteric and precise mathematical techniques as Monte Carlo and game theory' have played a very vital part in problem solving. Smith goes on to say that the H-bomb probably could not have been designed without the aid of Monte Carlo techniques.

However, this does not mean that think tanks are only concerned with nuclear weapons and strategic questions, Indeed, a great deal of their work is highly practical. For example, Rand, besides working on thermonuclear weapons and ballistic missiles has done a great deal of work on the recovery of circumlunar rockets; new materials and structures, such as titanium honeycomb sandwiches and metallic filaments, or whiskers as well as developing a whole new series of remarkable techniques for problem solving and long range forecasting. At Hudson some of the recently completed and current research projects include a study of the Choco Valley in Colombia with practical recommendations for its economic development; a study of New York City so as to determine how best to use subsurface areas for transportation and other sources, the means by which the City influences the activities of private parties and their interrelationship, particularly as regards City planning, ways to improve the City's high density, low income zones and alternative solutions to the problems of waste disposal and water and air pollution. The trend at Hudson, which like Rand has so far been identified with political–military studies is to move away from contracts with government agencies and to devote more attention to studies, such as the vast South American project, that are closely related to social and economical development. Although one or two think tanks, such as the Center for the Study of Democratic Institutions, are preoccupied with philosophical studies and seek to provide opportunities for free discussion of some of the great issues facing mankind, the majority of these research establishments are concerned with the physical and the behavioural sciences leading to discoveries, inventions and innovations as well as providing professional services for industrial and commercial managements and specialising in systems analysis and computer systems covering the widest fields of human activity.

The activities of GEC's Centre for Advanced Studies cover a very wide area and typical of the problems tackled for clients in a number of countries are:

How can a government ministry upgrade communications and transportation facilities through advanced systems engineering?

What modern action programs will best develop a new nation's human and natural resources?

What agricultural and food processing techniques can most rapidly increase world food production?

How can the president of a large international bank prepare for the social and technological environment of 1980?

How can a computerised management system improve a major industrial firm's operating efficiency?

Certain types of think tanks, e.g. the Samson Science Corporation, are solely concerned with business trends and have developed their own highly specialised techniques, in this instance, the input–output technique, to market research, product planning and corporate strategy with great success. Component input–output tables are now rightly regarded by business heads in the USA as essential tools in most enterprises involving manufactured goods. One of the key features of the Maptek Component Input–Output Service is its capability to simulate future alternate possible technological worlds and their impact on component markets. It can clearly answer questions such as 'What would be the market if the entire computer (or home entertainment, etc.) industry shifted totally to integrated circuits, or to large scale integration?'

For example, Arthur D. Little Inc., the most famous of the profit-making contract research centres, has come up with such money spinners as instant breakfast food, hot drink paper cups, missile fuels, low temperature cryostats and scores of others. Research on xerography, based on the inventor's (Chester Carlson) original concepts, began at Battelle-Columbus in 1944. The dry-copying process was developed to a point where a fully automatic electrostatic copying unit became commercially feasible. Titanium technology was pioneered at Battelle-Columbus and conceived by this think tank's technologists was the process used in making the reactor core in America's first atomic submarine. The Mellon Institute, now the Carnegie-Mellon University, has carried out many research projects for the benefit of the public, usually bearing on public health and include studies on smoke abatement, on industrial and urban dusts, on investigations into the cause and prevention of dental caries, studies in nutrition, a comprehensive investigation of sleep, research on tuberculosis and cancer.

Nothing is taken for granted in a think tank, every so-called fact and conclusion is challenged. At the Hudson Institute, one of America's most famous think tanks, this policy of challenging so-called proven facts is greatly encourged and Anthony Wiener, a prominent employee member of the Institute, goes so far as to say that it is the only trait that it really demands in a new recruit. Hudson Institute, a private, non-profit research organisation, has no obligations to stockholders, governments and other privileged bodies and enjoys complete independence. It is, therefore, free to look very critically at a situation and to tell its clients, whether it is a Federal Agency or a foreign government, what they see, irrespective of whether they want to hear it. This kind of refreshing candour is something that is seldom tolerated in the industrial or governmental research establishment.

The Different Disciplines of A Think Tank

Think tanks set out to solve far-reaching interconnected problems which would go unsolved either because they are impossible of solution without the use of the most powerful tools of mathematics and of computers or because they call for experimental work in a number of different fields that is quite beyond the resources of any single company, industry or even some countries. There is nothing rigidly professional about the think tank which is made up of many disciplines and where it is believed that the cross fertilisation of several academic skills is likely to be more fruitful than the straightforward method of plodding along with just one discipline. Modern think tanks aim at avoiding the 'compartmentalisation' of disciplines: projects may start in one department and spread rapidly across departmental boundaries and involve men of many skills. At Rand a project on strategic operations may start in the Economics or Social Science Departments, one on limited war in the Mathematics or System Operations Departments. To make the inter-disciplinary system work there needs to be a general freemasonry of knowledge and a readiness to cooperate; the political scientist is expected to know something about physics and the physicist to know something about the social sciences. It is realised that there are recesses of the mind that can only be explored by using new techniques and new approaches and the inter-disciplinary method, now commonplace in research establishments, is one of the most successful of these.

Very often solutions to problems are only made possible by evolving entirely new techniques which workers in several different academic and technological fields help to evolve. Many of the techniques now widely used by analysts in government, industry and the scientific community, e.g., system simulation methods, often involving the use of mathematical models; linear and dynamic programming, network theory; forecasting methods and decision theory; cost effectiveness analysis; sensitivity analysis and programme budgeting were tailor-made by Rand men—mathematicians, physicists, astronomers, lawyers, computer experts, accountants, psychologists and other specialists to fit specific problems.

The multi-disciplinary approach to problems originated at Rand which from its earliest days has found that a general looseness in organisation helped in the imaginative search for new ideas and relationships. In the Engineering Division roster of Rand one finds the occasional political scientist, astronomer, physiologist or psychologist while the Mathematics Division is headed by an astronomer–mathematician and uses the skills of the sociologist and the philosopher. A glance at Rand's Management Table makes fascinating reading, the titles of the Research Departments so provocatively different from what one might reasonably expect in a research establishment: Management Sciences; Engineering Sciences; Environmental Sciences; Social Science; System Sciences; Cost Analysis; Physics; Mathematics; Computer Sciences and Economics. The research staff of the Hudson Institute is made up of specialists in military operations and political anslysis; political scientists (who seem to predominate), mathematicians, specialists in ecology and biogeography, economists, the odd chemist, historians, political analysts, operations analysts, lawyers, psychologists and librarians.

More and more emphasis seems to be on the social scientist. Although in the early days of Rand there was considerable opposition to the idea of tying together the social science and the physical science sides of the Corporation in a mutually reinforcing way, there is no doubt that the scheme was highly successful and admittedly contributed a great deal in the vital hardware analyses of weapon systems. Although it might appear from this casual look at one of the most famous think tanks that theorists, specialists in the behavioural sciences, far outnumber the hard line of practical scientists, it has to be remembered that the nature of the problem dictates the kind of staff employed. Rand and Hudson are concerned mainly with policy research and regard their function primarily as giving research and advice to government. They see their main purpose as providing government agencies and other clients with the kind of assistance the President of the United States receives before making a decision; nobody tells the President what to do, but advisers do present alternative solutions and bases for choice which he is free to accept or reject. The studies carried out by these think tanks emphasise long range objections and/or crucial issues, especially those that are not currently regarded as pressing and immediate. The Hudson Institute claims that it attempts to act as a 'lobby for the future' or at least as a lobby for those important but not urgent issues.

Although it might appear that a political scientist with special training in international affairs would find few, if any, points of contact with a specialist in ecology and biogeography, a professional engineer with a background in building construction and a senior research chemist specialising in cancer chemotherapeutic agents, Hudson believe that this kind of pot-pourri produces the best and most enduring results. The history of science and technology is full of examples of great discoveries and inventions being made by people with little or no direct connections with the particular path of science leading up to the work, and one could mention here the work of chemists and physicists in the field of molecular biology.

In the field of technology there are numerous examples of inventions and discoveries made by people not even remotely connected with the projects in which they become involved. One only has to mention here the automatic knitting machine invented by the Reverend William Lee, a clergyman living quietly in a country vicarage at the time of Queen Elizabeth who got the idea through watching his wife knitting socks. Idly speculating on the speed with which his wife knitted he thought how much quicker a hundred or more needles would do the job. Lee built a machine and tried to interest people in the invention, but failed miserably and died unknown and unmourned in Belgium in 1610 to leave behind a brother who, in a few short years gained great success and considerable wealth from the Lee automatic knitting machine. Sturgeon, inventor of the electromagnet and commutator was a rough private soldier who became a natural philosopher by applying commonsense reason to little understood scientific phenomena. The solution to a problem does not always come from a logical scientific approach and creative achievements in science sometimes have odd beginnings. Henri Poincaré, the great mathematician, has told how he struggled hard but unsuccessfully to solve a difficult mathematical problem and finally left it to go on a geological excursion. Then some time later when he was thinking about something entirely alien to mathematics the solution to the problem 'appeared' in his mind.

The increasingly important role now played by the social scientist in think tanks concerned with policy research is an indication of the great emphasis placed on the inter-disciplinary approach. The fusing together of the social sciences with the physical sciences produced the new discipline–systems analysis —evolved out of earlier operations research techniques to cater for broader and more difficult problems than those traditionally covered by the term 'operations analysis'.

Whereas in operations research, mathematics or logical analysis can be applied to find more efficient ways of doing a job that is clearly defined, such as building a dry dock or a Polaris submarine, with systems analysis the analyst is faced not with one problem but a series of complex situations where the difficulty is to define the problem. The total analysis therefore becomes highly complex with much more emphasis placed on considered judgements than mathematical models. At Rand one of the most useful tools which it uses in tackling policy projects is operational gaming or simulation by groups of people chosen from different disciplines—economists, psychologists, biochemists, engineers, physicists, mathematicians, lawyers, etc.—who are free to apply their intuition and advice to common problems. It was the mathematician von Neumann who devised the theory of games to analyse situations in which two or more parties have interests that may be both cooperative and conflicting. But it was Rand who really turned an academic novelty into a workable technique that could be applied to a whole range of complex situations, such as radar search and prediction, to allocation of defence to targets of unequal value, to missile penetration aids, to the schedule of missile fire under enemy pindown, to anti-submarine warfare and to inspection for arms control. Systems analysis is now recognised as one of the most progressive approaches to difficult problems and the successes achieved in finding alternative methods of tackling them has only been made possible by the sparking off of one intellect against another, by focusing attention on conflict with a live, dynamic, intelligent and quick-reacting opponent.

The behavioural sciences, not necessarily because they are more vocal than the physical sciences but due rather to their more varied experiences and wider contact with life, are able to provide the flint that produces the right kind of spark at the right time. There is nothing long-haired and donnish about systems analysis. It is not just an academic exercise; it is essentially a technique with the widest applications to complex military, industrial and social problems, but to make it work a wide variety of professional skills is needed. While the importance of having available different disciplines to experiment with ideas about current problems is now recognised, the inter-disciplinary approach becomes even more important when dealing with the future and today a great deal of think tank work is concerned with the future. The military planners were the first to realise the importance of long range forecasting because of their growing concern about the possibility of their weapons systems becoming obsolete before they were ready for use. They looked hopefully at the think tanks, such as Rand and Hudson, to supply reliable forecasts of military situations that might arise, the balance of power in 10 and 20 years time, technological progress and new inventions that might change the pattern of weapons systems—a pretty formidable undertaking.

However, think tanks came up with some new ideas and refurbished a few old ones that held out the hope of scientific crystal gazing capable of producing forecasts of acceptable reliability. Even more important than the forecasting techniques that were evolved, think tanks developed an entirely new and revolutionary philosophy about the future. Instead of regarding it as fixed and something that man was unable to control, the view was encouraged that he was in charge of his own future and that the immediate job facing him was to define his goals and to work out the best way to reach them.

Today it is not the military who are the most active in taking advantage of the new science of futurology but industry. Vast sums of money are being spent on technological forecasting and in the United States it is estimated that some 600 firms spend £30 million a year on technological forecasting. Hard-headed business executives are only spending this kind of money because they are convinced that the future prosperity of their business can only be safeguarded by being one jump ahead of the competition, by their long range planners taking into account fast changing social conditions and the likelihood of new inventions and technologies altering the whole pattern of their industry, e.g. the impact of the zip-fastener on the button industry.

It was Rand's 'Report on a Long Range Forecasting Study' in 1964 that really focused attention on the subject and made it apparent that the future could be anticipated by applying certain simple and commonsense techniques to the particular problems. Basically these relied upon two methods of approach, the first one starting from the past and present and working towards the future and the second starting with the future and working backwards to the present.

The importance of having available in a research establishment several entirely different disciplines so that ideas can be exchanged and new avenues of thought and experience opened up as a result of discussion has been stressed in the case of think tanks concerned largely with policy research. The same holds good with those think tanks given over to the physical sciences. For this reason care is taken in the organisation of the centre to give the greatest degree of flexibility and freedom to the specialists in their work and to encourage interchanges of ideas so that where programmes call for contributions from inter-disciplinary skills these are readily available.

For example, it is not unusual at IITRI for the development of a new manufacturing process to involve chemists, metallurgists, electrical and mechanical engineers and computer scientists. The collective experience of specialists in the several branches of science and the diversity of technologies can very often enhance the chance of finding a solution to a tricky problem. Battelle was asked for a proposal to separate bark from wood chips and believed that the laboratory's mineral beneficiation group could be effective on this assignment. Minerals and wood technology seem far apart, but it was realised that this was a separation problem and as the minerals beneficiation group had achieved many outstanding successes in separation problems, this approach seemed justified. As it turned out the reasoning was correct and a successful method for separating bark from wood chips was developed by Battelle's minerals beneficiation group.

Frequent national and international conferences covering various technical areas are favoured by think tanks and at Midwest Research Institute (MRI)'s Spencer Auditorium, experts from all over the world are brought together to exchange fresh scientific information. Business executives and industrialists are shown, by means of symposia and interpretive seminars, the economic potentials arising out of the application to private industry of techniques and technology developed through research. At IITRI specialised skills as varied as non-destructive testing and information retrieval are often put at the disposal of commercial firms, government agencies and private industry. Since its founding in 1936 IIT Research Institute, formerly Armour Research Foundation of Illinois Institute of Technology, has completed more than 13,000 projects for over 3500 industrial and government clients.

The 400 or more think tanks in the USA cover practically every type of research; physical sciences, life science, industrial technology, economics, information retrieval, chemistry and nuclear energy. Some do management consulting and the behavioural sciences while others specialise in analysis, design and implementation of computer software systems and economic research.

A few are concerned with long range forecasting, although most consider this as an essential part of their work, while others are preoccupied with studies of social behaviour, education and religion or projects of political/military character.

3 THINK TANKS AND THE POWER GAME

Because of the growing complexity of many of the problems facing government agencies, the increasing pressure of new responsibilities imposed on them by environmental changes and the new technologies, policy making becomes increasingly difficult. Moreover, there is growing realisation in enlightened circles that problem solving often calls for advanced thinking of a type unfamiliar to officials working in government offices, many of whom are so bogged down with administrative details that they just cannot find sufficient time to give to the kind of enquiry and analysis essential to enable problems to be understood, let alone solved.

Under these conditions it is no surprise, therefore, that government agencies should look for help to the think tanks who not only have a great wealth of professional skills but enjoy uninterrupted time for research. Moreover these research organisations possess the most advanced tools of modern science, have first class computer support and are in a far better position to carry out the fundamental thinking so necessary before the right bases can be found for policy changes.

Information and data, while invaluable as raw material, is in itself quite useless unless properly interpreted. Although it is true to say that today's computer technology does mean new effectiveness for command and management—the old word 'GIGO' (acronym for 'garbage in, garbage out') no longer applying—in the last analysis everything depends on the use made of the information that is so carefully collected and processed and the recognition of its true significance. After all the value of Mendel's paper on the laws of inheritance was never recognised by his contemporaries! Knowledge is, of course, the essential ingredient of the mix, but it is not the only one.

Civilisation is suffering from a surfeit of information on every imaginable subject and the new science of cybernetics merely aggravates the position. More than one famous thinker has referred to the information overload, that fast accumulating byproduct of every major undertaking that constitutes a new form of pollution which no one knows how to get rid of without embarrassment. It all seems part of a wonderful game of 'kidology'. Think tanks have the measure of information; they are used to handling all and every kind of material, interpreting it where it is worth attention, sometimes ignoring facts, selecting and extracting the tiny drops of knowledge that may be present and really putting it to work.

Before answers are found for questions, there needs to be some examination of the questions themselves and the reasons why they should be answered at all: the specifications of the goals must preface any attempt to reach them: value preferences must be taken into account as well as the effect on the social structure of the technology's challenge to values. As Dr Emmanuel G. Mesthene of Harvard University (Program on Technology and Society) says:

'The effectiveness of system analysis (which is the Think Tank's usual approach) depends on having explicitly stated objectives and criteria of evaluations; to begin with the criteria and objectives of specific actions invariably relate to the society's system of values. That, incidentally is why the application of systems analysis meets with less relative success in educational or urban planning than in military planning: the value conflicts are fewer in the latter and the objectives and criteria easier to specify and agree on.'

However, it is not only in military planning that governments need the help of think tanks. Indeed, there would seem to be a growing need for their help in all those sections where the understanding of acute social problems, such as reducing unemployment, health, education, racial discrimination, pollution, alleviating poverty, etc., calls for study to understand causes and consequences before thinking about remedies. Too often in the history of nations vast sums have been spent on half baked schemes for social services which have never had a chance of achieving any real success because they are not prefaced by a thorough understanding of the problem before attempts were made to solve it.

In America a start has been made to tackle social problems in a rational way with the Institute for Urban Affairs: HUD established this body in 1967 and it is expected that other civilian agencies are likely to follow suit setting up 'within-the family' research institutes to give much needed first aid in policy planning.

In modern industry business opportunities have become increasingly difficult to identify and even more difficult to anticipate, yet the growth, if not the survival of a company depends on its ability to do this. It is in areas of great uncertainty where there is a continuing acceleration of product and market changes that many firms need a mix of skills not always at hand. This is where the techno-economic side of the independent research institute is able to give much needed first aid by looking at the problem objectively as only an outsider can do. Think tanks such as AD Little Incorporated and Booz, Allen and Hamilton specialise in this kind of work—a logical extension of management consulting.

The Growing Power of Think Tanks

As mentioned earlier in this book the think tanks are not without their critics and in many fields of government, industry and commerce there is bitter resentment of their growing power. In the main, criticism tends to fall into five main categories:

1 Because of their unique ability to reappraise the basic concepts of strategy and policy in the light of the latest scientific and technological information, their access to classified information and their ready acceptance by political leaders and top ranking military personnel think tanks are thought to be in too privileged a position to influence decisions affecting the welfare, security and freedom of the individual. The existence of an intellectual elite with the power to influence government decisions is in itself a direct threat to the democratic processes of government. If it is no longer possible to adjust decision making structures to the realities of the new technologies and increasing authority has to be delegated to bodies like the think tanks then if society is to have any chance of survival, some new system of government has to be worked out that will safeguard the vital freedoms of democracy.

2 Think tanks are said to be run by scholars so preoccupied with military forces and weapons, with strategy and policy planning as it affects the balance of power that the great social issues of our time, such as poverty, crime, racial discrimination, pollution, health and overpopulation are given a low priority in research programmes.

3 The quasi-academic atmosphere of the think tank is thought highly artificial and too much detachment is dangerous, and as a result the small band of physicists and social scientists, systems analysts, cyberneticists and mathematicians who attempt to explore major problems are out of touch and out of sympathy with the feelings and aspirations of the people they set out to help.

4 The formation and success of think tanks like Rand has, it is alleged, led to a government proliferation of research organisations and agencies responsible for defence, security and aerospace research. Their establishment tends to encourage government agencies to contract out an increasing volume of research tasks thereby adding appreciably to the cost of a project without contributing a great deal to the clarity of the solutions provided. In other words, it is claimed by the critics that the presence of research organisations tends itself to encourage fragmentary research which is often self-defeating. There are, unfortunately, too few think tanks of the high calibre of Rand.

5 Think tanks are considered too closely aligned with Big Business and as a result are looked at with suspicion by Trade Unions who mistrust their motives and believe that they constitute some new kind of threat to labour. What worries the Unions particularly is the way in which think tanks approach the future and their attempts to show the paths by which desired objectives can be achieved. It is realised that only the great power groups in society are in a position to fight politically for funds to subsidise think tanks and that this power needs to be checked.

Unfortunately think tanks suffer from too much secrecy, inevitable perhaps in view of the high percentage of scheduled work that is undertaken and the fact that much of their unscheduled research is incomprehensible to the vast majority of the public. The think tank's public image is shadowy and perhaps slightly sinister. As Bruce Smith says in his book about the Rand Corporation: 'One foreign observer remarked that representatives of certain US research organisations roam through the corridors of the Pentagon rather as the Jesuits through the courts of Madrid and Vienna three centuries ago'. Although these organisations say that one of their goals is 'to promote better communication and understanding among those working on public problems' to quote the Hudson Institute, there is a sad lack of adequate communication between the Research Institutes and the mass media which the public relies upon for its information. This may be because think tanks make unexciting material for the mass media. It would be difficult to convey the impression that the Hudson Institute's quiet retreat in the open, hilly country overlooking the Hudson River is the home of one of America's most famous think tanks or that the Rand Corporation's functional but unimpressive laboratories are any different from the dozens of aerospace consulting firms or hot electronics corporations that are to be found in California.

It is largely because of the think tank's poor public image, or lack of image, its hesitancy to be properly interpreted that there is so much misunderstanding about its function and mistrust of its motives. Although most of the criticism levelled against think tanks is directed towards those responsible for policy research, such as Rand and Hudson, it has to be realised that the majority of the research institutes in the United States that are labelled think tanks are concerned with less lofty research encompassing all facets of science and its application as well as pursuing programmes in fundamental research and education. Battelle Columbus is perhaps the best known of this type of physical science organisation.

Much of the uneasiness which exists about the future of the think tank as a new social organism stems from the unlimited freedom which the Rand type of organisation appears to enjoy, the fact that it is not accountable to any governing body, such as Board of Directors, stockholders, electorate or, in the case of a University, the Senate. It is, of course, true that most think tanks have a Board of Trustees made up of Presidents of large corporations and Universities, partners in prominent law firms, bankers and businessmen, but these have a fairly passive role to play in the general direction of the establishment and do not always exert control over the type of studies that are carried out.

The think tank pursues problems wherever they may lead 'without concern for special interests or bureaucratic positions on policy and technical issues' (Rand quote). It makes its own rules, assumes its own responsibilities, formulates its own code of ethics and approaches every problem with the cold objectiveness of the scientist committed only to intellectual quality. While independence and freedom from any kind of restraint are fine things in many ways, it carries with it some risk to the ideals of democracy which think tanks are allegedly out to safeguard—a risk of a new kind of scientific dictatorship which one day might direct the affairs of man. Maybe this is inevitable, but society is not yet ready to accept it!

Political leaders are becoming gradually aware of a general disillusionment with the inherited institutions and loss of confidence in the established systems with their drifting-into-whatever-may-come attitude. Think tanks represent a new and twentieth century opportunity to take a fresh look at the basic problems facing mankind using the latest tools of science, the new techniques and methodologies. The immense problem of pollution, which will soon be assuming menacing proportions threatening the health and future of life on this planet, is likely to be the first real challenge facing these establishments.

The new feeling, and this is shared particularly by the younger generation, is that because think tanks represent the best brains of the nation, owe allegiance to no one except their own scientific principles, enjoy a large amount of freedom, they are in a better position to restore man's authority over the technosphere than any other body of people. For this reason there is an increasing pressure from a number of directions to look to them for help and to study if not to follow their advice.

Because of the readiness with which think tanks are being listened to by those in authority, the eagerness with which they are consulted and their presence in the corridors of power, Big Business is becoming apprehensive about the future of its own role in influencing policy decisions, zealous of the challenge which think tanks are making to its established R & D leadership. It is even being whispered that the future might see R & D being taken out of the control of Big Business (in the United States some 300 companies do 90 per cent of the country's research) and contracted out to think tanks such as the General Electric's TEMPO, which are well equipped to do the work and to feed the manufacturing industries with sufficient innovations, discoveries, technological transfers and business strategies to keep the economy happy, and at a greatly reduced cost to the nation. At the present time the production of technical knowledge far outstrips its use and what is most urgently needed is not more innovations and inventions, since the backlog is already formidable, but new means of communication and a better understanding between businessmen and intellectuals. As Charles N. Kimball, President of the Midwest Research Institute says, this is where the 'soft' scientists, the economists, social and political scientists and the psychologists who make up the think tank team can play a useful part in helping to improve the general acceptance of new ideas and to broaden the base of research.

In this way it would not only be the giant corporations who would benefit from the R & D effort, but industry at large. This is not entirely a pipedream. The think tanks are here; they are becoming more powerful, their reputation stands high, based as it is on outstanding achievements in the fields of science and technology and they enjoy the growing confidence of the public agencies. There is a growing awareness that much of the vast expenditure on R & D is wasted, the return on capital too low to justify spending at the present rate and a great deal of work is duplicated. There is no reason why such a framework should not work for science. The fact that it smacks of a totalitarian regime is not in itself a damning enough indictment. Think tanks need not become the tools of State, rather partners in helping to run it.

There is, of course, a risk, although not a serious one, that advisory bodies such as think tanks may become impatient with the ineptitude of our policy makers and try to take away from us all the responsibility for making decisions, leaving us as a kind of slave society. Indeed, some scientists such as Bronowski, are really afraid that this may happen—perhaps it is the price civilisation will have to pay in order to prevent it from devouring itself!

4 THE DIFFERENT KINDS OF NON-PROFIT AMERICAN THINK TANKS

The not-for-profit think tanks differ considerably in origins, growth, patterns, organisation, fields of specialisation, disciplines, staff size and policies. With the possible exception of one or two establishments, such as the Center for Strategic and International Studies, the Center for the Study of Democratic Institutions and Harvard University Program on Technology and Society, most of the not-for-profit research institutes rely to a large extent on American government support in the form of sponsored research contracts. For instance, some three quarters of the projects carried out by the research laboratories, such as Battelle, IITRI, Stanford, Franklin and Midwest to mention only five of the largest independent research institutes are on behalf of federal agencies and with most of them the emphasis is on applied research and development and not basic research.

With some of these research institutes where there is close affiliation with a university there is an increasing nervousness about heavy involvement with defence and this is particularly noticeable where the institute is situated on the university campus. Some universities, notably Harvard, have for some time now refused classified research. However, without contracts from the big spenders, such as the Department of Defense (DoD), National Aeronautics and Space Administration (NASA), the Atomic Energy Commission (AEC) and the Department of Health, Education and Welfare (HEW) many of the American think tanks would be hard put to it to keep going. However, with a big cut in government spending on defence research, think tanks are building up their techno-economic departments so as to attract more clients from industry and commerce.

4

There are, of course, some think tanks that work exclusively for the United States Government, such as the Institute for Defense Analyses (IDA), while others like Rand and Hudson, although depending on the Government for the bulk of their contracts do work under grants from various outside concerns.

These institutes are known as not-for-profit establishments because they are not required to pay Federal Income Tax, the Internal Revenue Service categorising them as tax exempt. Each institute is controlled by a Board of Governors or Trustees which is responsible to the staff and to the public for its operation. The Board of Trustees usually elects the institute's officers; provides general policy guidance; amends the corporate by-laws, as appropriate; provides specific approval on certain key actions; and retains power to dissolve the organisation.

The not-for-profit research institutes are unique to the United States and there is nothing like them anywhere else in the world. Certainly the United Kingdom has no establishment that even remotely resembles a think tank, the British attitude towards R & D being rigidly professional. The idea that a political scientist or a sociologist might work alongside a mathematician, as at the Rand Corporation, in solving a problem seems quite absurd to the majority of researchers and there is general resistance to the idea, which is also favoured at Rand, that there are no boundaries to individual areas of research. The British scientific worker likes boundaries clearly defined.

In the UK research and development are carried out by private industry, university, technical college and by the chain of scientific and technological establishments that come under the Ministry of Technology. When this Ministry was set up in 1964 it took over many of the functions and most of the resources of the Department of Scientific and Industrial Research including the National Physical Laboratory, the National Engineering Laboratory and also assumed responsibility for the National Research Development Corporation and for the UK Atomic Energy Authority. Through its chain of industrial liaison centres normally based on Colleges of Advanced Technology and regional and area technical colleges Mintech keeps in contact with local firms, particularly the smaller one, encouraging them to make greater use of existing scientific and technical knowledge. The Ministry's strong emphasis is on engineering and most of the 18 establishments are strongly biased towards it, technology being catered for through the 43 research associations working alongside industry.

The trouble with Mintech's R & D policy and particularly with its new grandiose scheme for setting up a British Research and Development Corporation to take over from the existing establishments and to turn the direction of the Ministry's research away from government directives towards serving social and economic needs is that it is Whitehall directed, subject to paralysing bureaucratic control, overstaffed with civil servants without any real knowledge or feeling for industry and lacking the independence and flexibility of commercial R & D establishments.

Faced with a disappointing return on Britain's national spending on R & D it is little wonder that people both inside and outside of government should question the wisdom of trying to make a government oriented research organisation work alongside industry and expecting it to 'encourage and support the development and technological improvement in industry for the benefit of the UK economy, and carry out research and development for this purpose, both itself and in collaboration with industry and on repayment.' (*Industrial Research and Development in Government Laboratories: A New Organisation for the Seventies*. Ministry of Technology, HMSO.)

The great weakness of the present set-up is that as the Green Paper says 'no government department can decide centrally what research programmes are best designed to serve the needs of industry.'

British industry has never yet been very impressed with the industrial awareness of those who control government R & D policies or with their ability to work out any straightforward and simple method of contractual relationship which will guarantee to clients high quality research within competitive cost and time limitations; in other words to give the same kind of service as the independent research institutes do in the United States.

The Labour Government's ambition to put its research establishments on a contractual commercial basis and to justify projects in terms of what they are worth to the customer gives one the impression that those designing the new R & D policies had in mind the independent research institutes in America, such as Battelle Memorial Institute, which with a budget approaching $100 million and a professional staff of 6700 scientists, engineers, economists and supporting personnel might be said to compete in size with any government laboratory in the UK. Indeed, all of the Ministry of Technology's industrial research establishments (five of them) employ only

1450 professional staff and cost some £11·4 million to keep going. The Atomic Energy Authority's Research Group Establishments at Harwell and Culham Laboratory also employ 1450 professional staff and cost the British taxpayer £19·5 million.

Although much of the growth and prosperity of the American think tanks stem from the vast US Government research programme, mostly on weaponry and aerospace projects (some 40–75 per cent of the total volume of work undertaken by the research institutes can be traced to contracts from the federal agencies) there is still left a fairly big margin for industry to take up. However, even with the big cutback in Government spending on defence, security and projects like Apollo and dwindling support from the foundations, there is no reason to believe that the think tanks will not be able to survive. Their value to industry is now fully recognised and their ability to solve the social and economic problems facing the nation assures them of continuing support in the future. They have, in fact, become indispensable.

British R & D establishments rely entirely on government work. They are 100 per cent a taxpayer liability. Because of their peculiar structure and organisation, the fact that they have grown up to give government the kind of scientific help it needs, it is difficult to see how they can, at least for many years, be in a position to bridge the gap between science and industry and to offer the British manufacturer the kind of all round service that his opposite number in America expects from the laboratory think tanks.

There are seven main categories of not-for-profit institutes in the United States, although it needs to be stressed that there is some overlapping of responsibilities, none of the groupings being watertight compartments. Some of the contract research institutes also carry out business studies and long range forecasting as well as work in the physical sciences, while there are advisory corporations and centres of research which do both.

1 Independent contract research institutes like Battelle, IITRI, Stanford, Midwest, Southern, Franklin, North Star, Triangle, Denver, etc. concentrate on applied research and development. They have well equipped laboratories and experimental workshops and employ highly qualified professional staff in the physical sciences, technology, engineering and some life sciences. The aims and objects of these organisations have been variously described by officials of the institutes,

but all are agreed that their primary purpose is to do research in the public interest, achieving these ends by 'bridging a gap between the scholarly exploration of the academic world and the technology needs of business, industry and government.' Essentially the contract research institutes are clinics of technology where, in the words of the Southwest Research Institute, 'basic findings are translated into products and processes which are useful to the public and profitable to sponsors.

2 Advisory Corporations such as Rand, Hudson and the Institute for Defense Analysis (IDA) who provide the federal agencies with independent and objective sources of analyses, evaluations and advice. Studies carried out by these establishments attempt to reflect an examination of all relevant data and hypotheses and point out policy or procedural alternatives for consideration by the government decision makers in evaluating the options available to them. A great deal of the work done by the advisory corporation is classified although both Hudson and Rand, particularly the former, are tending to become more diversified by taking on projects not directly concerned with defence and security. On the other hand, IDA works exclusively for the United States Government.

3 Institutes like the Center for Strategic and International Studies which try to advance the understanding of international policy issues through inter-disciplinary study of emerging world problems, and their primary work is the preparation of studies, reports and books on international issues. Organisations such as this do not take government or industry contracts nor receive any government funding in any form, sources of support being confined to the foundations, corporations and gifts from individuals.

4 Institutes which investigate economic, political and social trends and examine philosophical questions, the best known being the Institute for Policy Studies, the Center for Research on Conflict Resolution, the Center for the Study of Democratic Institutions, Harvard University Program on Technology and Society and the Hoover Institution of War, Revolution and Peace, etc.

5 Institutes which set out to organise systematic and comprehensive studies of the long range future, e.g. the Institute

for the Future in Connecticut and Resources for the Future (RFF) which specialises in objective research on critical issues as they affect future national developments.

6 Small organisations such as Spindletop in Kentucky and Gulf South Research Institute, Baton Rouge, which have a strong regional bias and carry out research in several fields to further the economy of their state. Gulf gives as its primary objective to add to man's fund of knowledge and to enhance the scientific, eduational and economic development of the region.

7 Institutes such as the one at Princeton, New Jersey, for Advanced Study which is devoted to the encouragement, support and patronage of learning—of science in the old, broad, undifferentiated sense of the word. The Institute for Advanced Study was founded in 1930 by a gift of Mr Louis Bamberger and his sister Mrs Felix Field. It has three schools: a School of Mathematics, a School of Natural Sciences and a School of Historical Study. Unlike most of the institutes mentioned in previous categories this one is without any experimental facilities.

5 NON-PROFIT-MAKING THINK TANK LABORATORIES

According to a fairly recent survey there are 280 independent non-profit research or development institutes in America, this number taking in all kinds of miscellaneous organisations including some private foundations. However, there are 60 contractual non-profit research institutes which might be termed 'think tank laboratories', most of them founded by private interests with private funds. Practically all these establishments are independent in so far as they have complete freedom to accept or reject outside contracts, final selection being left to the staff. The criterion is that the work in question must conform with the institute's programme or that it is to be of such a nature that it offers scope for the special aptitudes and skills of the institute.

Although enjoying the independence of the average non-profit research institute, three of the most famous think tank laboratories are contractual managers for US Government research centres: the Franklin Institute manages the Navy's Centre for Naval Analysis: Battelle Memorial Institute operates the Pacific Northwest Laboratories for the Atomic Energy Commission (AEC) and IITRI is contractual manager of the Air Force Electromagnetic Compatibility Analysis Center. This, of course, is in line with American policy to reduce as far as possible federal bureaucracy by putting R & D to outside research bodies rather than building up massive Government laboratories. It is interesting to note here that the American Manhattan Engineer District operates none of its own laboratories with Government personnel but functions solely by contract with private organisations.

The rapid growth of the think tank laboratories is due to three main factors:

1 The policy of the US Government to carry out as far as possible massive R & D programmes by contract (or

grant) using independent research centres and the staff and facilities best suited to the work. While the bulk of it is allocated to private industry, universities and colleges, quite a healthy proportion finds its way to the independent research institutes.

2 Industry's increasing awareness of the commercial value of creative research and recognition of the importance of the research institutes in being able to supplement their own R & D.

3 Funding of more long term research projects by the various foundations.

Their survival in the highly competitive world of contractual research rests entirely on their ability to produce results within the time limits set by their sponsors and to reduce costs so that fees are well in keeping with acceptable standards. They are able to achieve all this because of their research competence and flexibility of structure, plus the fact that they can apply varied disciplines to complex problems and have at hand all the skills and expertise necessary for the work. Often they are better fitted to tackle difficult assignments in applied research than the universities because of their ability to organise staff on less rigid lines.

Research institutes are primarily concerned with creative research, justification for their existence lying in their unique ability 'to bridge the gap between the kind of basic research performed in universities and the product-oriented research done in industry laboratories. This is a broad area—one in which the multi-disciplinary approach is especially beneficial.' (Gibson, Stanford Research Institute).

Projects range from relatively simple tasks, such as the development of a new type of silica insulator calling for specialised knowledge in the field of ceramics, to exceedingly complex sequences of activities. As the hardware of war has become more sophisticated and complex so has the need for R & D at the various stages of development become greater. Not only have the number of parts involved in any one device multiplied many thousands of times, but new systems call for new materials and new methods of assembly. In general, the research institutes are more concerned with projects which are fairly clearly defined than long term research and it is organisations like Rand, System Development Corporation and other advisory corporations who become heavily involved with programmes, some of which may take several years to complete.

The institutes do not engage in routine commercial testing and analysis, consulting and market research or compete directly with the commercial testing laboratories and the consultants. The not-for-profit institutes have been criticised both by industrial and commercial laboratories as enjoying an unfair advantage in not paying income tax, charging excessive fees and exorbitant overheads, poaching the best brains from the universities and from industry by offering higher rates of pay than are customary and carrying out research management and other fringe activities outside the realm of creative research.

There is some confusion over tax relief which is only granted where the research institute undertakes work of a non-commercial character. Where a project results in a proprietary advantage to the sponsor then tax has to be paid. Tax exemption calls for a highly complicated and costly accounting system and because of this some research institutes decline to do work that may possibly mean that they become liable to tax. It is doubtful, therefore, whether in the long run this tax relief benefit is, in fact, a real advantage.

A research institute, such as Battelle which is easily the largest, does both research management and management of research, both being regarded as essential parts of problem solving. Research management analyses both short range and long range needs; relates these to markets, competition, technological advances; determines manpower and budget to be applied, establishes priority of research projects. Management of research is generally concerned with efficient administration of specific projects aimed at reaching the goals of research management.

There is growing pressure from a number of sources, including government, to force the think tank laboratories to keep to R & D and not to meddle with management consulting in any way unless they are prepared to lose their tax-free exemption. One or two of the institutes, such as IITRI, which has an excellent reputation for this kind of service has now set up its own for-profit commercial organisation so as to give its industrial clients what it considers to be a valuable service, offering a whole range of management services including product diversification, acquisition analysis, organisation and marketing, etc. Another criticism levelled against the think tank laboratories is that some of them lean too heavily on the universities and benefit unfairly from the many valuable services which they are able to offer and which are unavailable to industry and the commercial laboratories. A few of the institutes, such as Denver, form an integral part of the university. Many of the personnel at Denver Research Institute serve as professors in their respective departments at the University which itself provides the academic environment for all the research that is carried out. This role includes the maintenance of many facilities, such as the library, laboratories and the computer centre which is the nucleus of all the work done in the computer science field.

Other research institutes have close ties with universities but not actually part of them. For example, Research Triangle Institute in North Carolina is strategically sited within a short distance of the state's three leading universities and although it leans heavily on them it was established as an independent corporate entity and operates under a separate Board of Governors with its own full time staff. At the same time RTI makes use of the IBM 360/75 at the Triangle Universities Computation Center, the largest computer network of its kind in the United States. RTI also shares in the libraries of the three universities. Many other research institutes such as Battelle Memorial, while not affiliated to a university, have a friendly working relationship.

The close ties existing between universities and not-for-profit research institutes are highly advantageous to both organisations. A university like Stanford shares a great deal of the reflected glory of its world-famous institute, its staff welcome the opportunity to be called in as consultants on specific problems and graduates look forward to the time when they may be offered highly paid jobs by the institute. From the institute's viewpoint, a university provides additional research and consultative facilities, makes available excellent libraries and other specialised services which might be difficult, and certainly costly, to find elsewhere. Altogether it is a very convenient partnership and it is hardly surprising therefore that both industrial and commercial laboratories should be envious and a little sore about it!

It is said by some that the independent not-for-profit research institutes are unnatural growths living in the artificial atmosphere created by massive government aid in the form of defence and other federal agency contracts and that once these conditions are removed, the plants are sure to wither and die. There is, of course, a great deal of truth in this rather picturesque statement, but unless a government builds up a massive and highly expensive R & D colossus able to handle all the nation's scientific requirements, contracting out becomes absolutely essential. Moreover with big new projects, such as aerospace research and crisis-loaded social problems like pollution and urban development, highly specialised services are needed. Government research stations and laboratories are already overloaded with work, the universities committed to basic research and not really interested in technology, and profit-motivated industry reluctant to spend a great deal of time and money on research programmes that show little promise of materialising into hardware. Every encouragement has, therefore, to be given to research institutes which are able to handle the many straightforward research tasks from which the agencies contract out. Indeed, without this kind of work many of the institutes would hardly be able to survive as some, such as Stanford Research Institute, gross tens of millions of dollars a year.

There is nothing particularly novel about contracting out government research. In 1830 the United States Government placed its first contract—the investigation of steam boiler explosions—with the Franklin Institute and its report formed the basis of new legislation governing 'boilers and engines of vessels propelled in the whole or part by steam' in 1838. After the successful conclusion of this project the Franklin Institute became heavily involved in federal research: a study of building stone from Pennsylvania and Delaware quarries for use in the construction of breakwaters and other public works, information on telegraphic communications investigation of an explosion of new 12-inch guns on the USS *Princeton*. More and more The Franklin Institute responded to federal appeals for help.

However, when looked at in terms of actual percentage of the American R & D's budget, the research institute's contribution is a drop in the ocean, a mere 1·25 per cent. Yet for this small investment these organisations have not only produced an impressive list of inventions, innovations and discoveries and contributed substantially to the fund of knowledge in a number of directions, but they have been a great help in furthering the economic development of their regions. From these think tanks have come the evolution of the Xerox process by Battelle Memorial, the basic development and application of magnetic recording at Illinois Institute of Technology (IITRI), formerly Armour; research in techno-economics and long range planning at Stanford; synthetic rubber and industrial hygiene at Mellon, the world's first deep diving submarine at Southwest; pioneer work in solid lubricants and metal fatigue at Midwest. The list is certainly impressive by any standards.

A research institute adds a good deal of prestige to a region, attracts to it science oriented industry, provides good employment opportunities for its graduates from the university and stimulates local economy through studies of its resources and by applying scientific methods to the study of regional problems.

The importance of a research institute is now fully recognised by progressive businessmen in the region, most of whom appreciate the value of technology based research in producing new knowledge, new products and new processes, so providing new opportunities for industry and commerce.

When Stanford Institute was formed in 1946 the University was careful to mention the 'western' nature of the new Research Institute, a tactful and necessary admission as leading industrialists of southern and central California and of the Pacific Northwest had cooperated in organising the new entity rather than creating separate and small institutes in various localities. One of the first pieces of research carried out some 20 years ago by SRI was on tallow to find new uses for this important by-product on behalf of Tallow Research Inc., an organisation of Californian origin. This programme of research resulted in a number of important discoveries, some of which formed the basis for patents and usable processes taken up on a royalty basis by various firms. The project soon became self-supporting and still continues to this day on behalf of Tallow Research Inc.

Another early research project undertaken by SRI on the spinnability of cotton was designed to help the Californian cotton spinners to produce a better quality fibre for the spinning mills.

In those early days of SRI much of the research had a distinct Californian flavour and this was very necessary in order to retain the interest and enthusiasm of the early sponsors. Today Stanford, while still very much concerned with the prosperity of the region, has grown to be an international organisation; one fifth of its research activities are, in fact, of an international character through its operating bases in Zurich, Tokyo and Stockholm.

Although Stanford has been foremost in research in the hard sciences it specialises in the interactions between science, technology and society and was one of the early pioneers of long range technological forecasting. Stanford offers industry and commerce a long range planning service that has a high reputation.

The Midwest Research Institute provides another good example of a think tank formed originally to help in the economic and social growth of a region—the Middle West. It was founded in 1944 by a group of civic and industrial leaders in Kansas City and some 300 companies, individuals and foundations contributed funds to start the Institute. In its early days many of the research projects undertaken by MRI were of great concern to the Middle West and success in tackling these gave the Institute not only firm establishment in the eyes of local businessmen but helped to give it a national reputation. Typical of these first problems were evaluation of the potential for new scientifically based enterprises in the Midwest: critical review and market evaluation of equipment used in pollution control and waste disposal; analyses of food processing industries in Iowa and plant locating cost analyses for attracting new plants.

Most of the new Institutes founded since 1959 followed the pattern of SRI and Midwest in seeking originally to further regional aims. For instance Research Triangle Institute in North Carolina is described by its President as participating 'in a multi-pronged effort to affect the character of a region, and thereby to change the character of its economic base, through an order of magnitude expansion of the region's scientific and technical activity, so that it can attain a position in the national research scene'.

Spindletop, a small contract research institute formed in 1961 was specifically designed to help the Commonwealth of Kentucky and, in fact, the State helped it along by purchasing for it a new, modern research facility and a 130 acre estate near Lexington. One of the first projects which Spindletop carried out was for the Kentucky Chamber of Commerce on behalf of the Kentucky distilling industry to find out the effects of Kentucky's 10 cent per proof gallon production tax on that industry's operations and the state economy. The report of this project was used extensively in preparing for the repeal of the tax by the 1966 General Assembly. This institute is particularly active in the field of national resources and projects have been carried out on oil and gas exploration in Kentucky by prominent oil firms, and already these companies have drilled between 50 and 100 deep wells, several of which are producing.

Probably one of the best examples of think tanks helping in regional development is afforded by the Nebraska experiment, a novel plan for economic growth, the lynch pin of the plan being to make available to local industries the patent rights covering processes for the commercial utilisation of the state's agricultural products of which it has a large surplus.

The research projects were all designed to produce commercially viable products assigned to a number of think tanks and profit-making contract research establishments, such as Foster D. Snell and Bjorksten. These organisations set out to do four things:

1 Utilise Nebraksa's agricultural raw materials for industrial purposes.
2 Carry out product research rather than process or production research.
3 Produce commercial results from the applied research in as short a time as possible, rather than fundamental or long range research.
4 Produce results that would have a significant favourable impact on Nebraska if successful.

Choice of research laboratories was based upon their pre-eminence in areas promising maximum return for the state's research dollar. One choice was the US Department of Agriculture's Western Regional laboratories for research on alfalfa-protein separation. Five industrial laboratories were selected: Midwest Research Institute (research in corn, castor beans, soyabeans and wheat); Southwest Research Institute (corn research); Bjorksten Research Laboratories (corn starch research); Institute of Paper Chemistry (dry milled corn starch research); and the Foster D. Snell subsidiary of Booz-Allen Applied Research (industrial utilisation of tallow and lard).

Up to date the research has produced a number of very promising new products. For example, Midwest has come up with a water soluble packaging film; Foster D. Snell with sucrose esters for cosmetics and Southwest has developed a process to make corn derived ethyl alcohol, and it looks like being a sound investment for Nebraska.

A look at the layout of any one of the major think tanks shows at a glance the wide spectrum of disciplines that are covered and the emphasis given to the breaking down of the artificial barriers existing among the various scientific disciplines and engineering and among the physical and life sciences. The early think tanks were mainly concerned with the physical sciences and engineering and their staff consisted of chemists, physicists and engineers. Now the institutes have added biological and medical sciences, techno-economics, management sciences and psychology. As would be expected some degree of specialisation is found in most establishments and this is generally recognised as an important factor in attracting new contracts.

For example, the Franklin Research Institute which has inherited a great deal of the Franklin Institute's interest in mechanical engineering has a strong bias towards engineering projects and systems science. As a result its services are in great demand not only by the Federal agencies, including the aerospace research organisations, but to an increasing extent by industry. Indeed, Dr Wynn Laurence Lepage in his New-comer Address (26 November 1968) predicted that over the next decade the Franklin Research Institute would be the nucleation centre of many new industrial corporations. Although Battelle Memorial's activities embrace virtually all facets of science and its applications, it has, since its foundation 35 years ago been a pioneer in materials technology, including the development of new materials, particularly titanium, for service at the extremes of temperature and pressure typical of space-age applications. It has also pioneered in the application of economics to industrial research in the physical sciences.

IITRI is exceptionally strong in chemical, metallurgical and ceramic processes techniques and its high reputation in these fields, particularly in the development of advanced control techniques in the basic industries, attracts to it a number of industrial as well as government contracts.

Southwest Research Institute in Texas is world known for its department of engines, fuels and lubricants evaluation and provides research and development services for every major manufacturer, government agency and refinery in the auto-motive field in the United States. The department also carries out research and development studies for 41 organisations in 16 foreign countries.

All the work undertaken by the research institute is on a contract basis, the institute providing services and facilities for the conduct of the research project and agreeing to devote as much time and effort to the investigation as is deemed necessary for its fruitful conclusion. The essential elements of most contracts include four main items:

1 Definition of the scope of the research.
2 Specification of data for starting the research, time and cost estimates, terms of payment. At the Franklin Research Laboratories the sponsor is charged only with the costs incurred for his project and these include direct project expenses and a proportionate share of indirect costs.

Direct project expenses include charges for staff members directly participating in the project, charges for expendable and non-expendable supplies and materials and other costs directly assignable to the project. The sponsor's proportionate share of overhead expenses covers those costs whose direct accounting is impractical or uneconomical. A fixed fee is taken upon the total cost.

3 The stipulation that the sponsor receive all rights to results obtained, proprietory to his probject.

4 The stipulation not to disclose to third parties the scope of the project or the results of the research work without the consent of the sponsor or until such information is in the public domain.

Why does a firm use contract research when it has its own research facilities? One answer is that it only does so when it wants information in areas outside its usual fields of interest. To give a simple example, an engineering firm might be involved in a big project where the success of a certain mechanism depends on the use of a new type of lubricant that will remain stable at unusually high temperatures and pressures. The development of such a lubricant might well present serious problems to the management as the type of research needed is outside the experience and capability of the firm's scientific staff and, even if attempted and the research were successful, more essential and probably more profitable work would have to be sacrificed. Another important reason why the firm should turn to the research institute for help is that it might lack the special equipment needed to do the work and has not at hand the testing facilities so essential to its success.

By calling in outside research, such as the Southwest Institute in Texas, which has the largest independent fuels and lubricants laboratory in the world, the firm knows that greater success is likely to be achieved in a much shorter time than would be possible in its own laboratories. Moreover Southwest's engineers not only devise tests to ensure lubricant efficiency under all conditions of use, but have long experience in determining specifications for new and untried compounds. This seems to make a great deal of sense.

Think tank laboratories are highly selective and do not take on any assignment without a good deal of thought. They have first to be convinced that the project is worth while, involves creative research and not just routine testing and analysis, arouses the enthusiasm and continuing interest of the research staff who will be called in to do the work and is calculated to make some useful contribution to industry, the community or to mankind. This all sounds rather idealistic but it is a fact that the research institutes, even in this highly commercial age, try to retain the original idea of doing research in the public interest.

Not all the projects tackled by these think tank laboratories are big ones, but big or small they need to present something of a challenge to the project team. What is particularly impressive about the work of these institutions is not so much the volume, although this is considerable, but the wide range of disciplines engaged and the catholicity of the subjects. For example, the Southwest Research Institute, which is fairly typical of the medium sized think tank laboratory, dealt with 712 projects in 1968 covering project areas such as encapsulation research and development; hydrophilic films for improved desalination processes; new uses for sulphur and the exploration of new techniques for sulphur recovery; industrial air and water pollution control; research related to the undesirable emissions from vehicular power plants; study of the free radical species present in tobacco smoke and tar and their significance as carcinogenic agents; automatic blood pressure monitoring apparatus and other bio-engineering studies; engineering physics as applied to problems in the natural gas industry; advanced methods for radio direction finding; non-destructive testing; ocean engineering in the areas of submarine design; structural dynamics relating particularly to new composite materials; materials research as applied to modern nuclear power problems; fuels and lubricants and engine systems; fire technology and operations research. An impressive list!

Some innovations of the type which might be termed technological trivia inevitably result from certain research programmes. For example, in its work on finding new uses for sulphur, Southwest came up with a whole catalogue of commercially attractive ideas, such as a new and highly superior sulphur based traffic marking paint which is now being marketed by a large chemical manufacturer on a national scale. However, it is not felt that innovations themselves, although useful and profitable to their sponsors, provide sufficient justification for undertaking R & D work on the scale favoured at a research institute.

America's Most Famous Think Tank Laboratories

Name	Date founded	1967 Budget ($ million)	Full time staff	Status	Main fields of interest
Battelle Memorial	1927	93·5	6500	Non-profit	Chemistry and chemical engineering, process and physical metallurgy, mechanical engineering, physics, nuclear science, life sciences. Especially known for metallurgy and materials engineering.
Stanford Research Institute	1946	55·0	3000	Non-profit	Physical, biological and social sciences, engineering and the mechanical arts. Best known for work in economics and electronics.
Arthur D. Little, Inc.	1886	35·0	1400	Profit-making	Research and development, life sciences, management sciences and engineering. Specialising in industrial, physical, pharmaceutical and analytical chemistry and management sciences.
Illinois Institute of Technology (IITRI)	1936	29·0	1900	Non-profit	Ceramics, chemistry, chemical engineering, computer sciences, electronics, life sciences, mechanics, metals, physics, gas dynamics, space sciences.
Franklin Institute Research Laboratories (Part of the Franklin Institute founded in 1824)	1946	7·0	350	Non-profit	Research and development for industry and government covering the physical and life sciences. Environmental science and engineering.
Southwest Research Institute	1944	13+	1000	Non-profit	Ocean science and engineering, encapsulation, biosciences and bio-engineering, highway safety, non-destructive testing; fire technology, structure research, fuels and lubricants, aerospace and communications. US Army Fuels and Lubricants Research Laboratory.

America's Most Famous Think Tank Laboratories (contd.)

Name	Date founded	1967 Budget ($ million)	Full time staff	Status	Main fields of interest
Midwest Research Institute	1944	5·4+	380	Non-profit	Physical sciences, engineering, biological and life sciences, social sciences and economics. Major interests in chemistry, including surface chemistry, energy conversion and solid state chemistry.
Houston Research Institute	1963	750,000	50	Profit-making	Engineering and design, research and development, applied computer science, economics, marketing and management.
Spindletop Research Institute	1961	1·2	100	Non-profit	Industrial sciences and environmental sciences, communications and economic development. Increasing emphasis on pollution studies.
North Star Research & Development Institute	1963	740,000	45	Non-profit	Electrometalling, electrical engineering, polymer chemistry and chemical engineering. Biological sciences, economics and psychology.
Research Triangle Institute	1959	3·8	274	Non-profit	Research in natural sciences, e.g. biologically active natural compounds, fundamental studies of the chemistry and physics of polymers; operations research and economics.
Gulf	1965	850,000	40	Non-profit	Physical sciences, life sciences, engineering, economics and human resources research; environmental sciences and eco-engineering.
Denver Research Institute	1947	6·2	480	Non-profit	Chemistry, electronics, electromagnetic propagation, industrial economics, mechanics, metallurgy and physics, chemical engineering projects include oil shale technology. Also specialised subjects include metal hydrides, rare earth technology, nuclear instrumentation.

America's Most Famous Think Tank Laboratories (contd.)

Name	Date founded	1967 Budget ($ million)	Full time staff	Status	Main fields of interest
Bjorksten Research Laboratories	1944	1·5	100	Profit-making	Metallurgy, biochemical sciences, theoretical and applied physics, inorganic and high temperature materials and organic and polymer chemistry.
Booz-Allen Applied Research	1955	10·0	670	Profit-making	Physical sciences and engineering, biological life sciences and economics. Specialises in management consulting, computer systems.
Cornell Aeronautical Laboratory	1946	22·3	1340	Non-profit	Aeronautical sciences and related fields (wholly owned subsidiary of Cornell University).
Mellon Institute	1913	6·2	1800	Non-profit	Biochemistry and molecular biology, environment and public health, structure and properties of organic materials. Emphasis on long range projects rather than specific problem solving. (Mellon Institute has now become Carnegie/Mellon University.)
University City Science Research Institute	1964	150,000	5	Non-profit	Physical sciences and life sciences (smallest of the research institutes.)

6 PROFIT-MAKING THINK TANK LABORATORIES

On the profit-making side of the contract research business there are a number of American companies and one or two English ones which may be classed as think tanks. It is significant that the largest and most successful of these organisations is heavily involved in management consulting, offering industry and commerce a new deal in scientific management as well as a highly organised and efficient research service. There is a strong feeling that as industry has such a large backlog of inventions, discoveries, innovations and technological transfers from which to choose that its immediate need is guidance as how best to make use of this rich inheritance.

Management consultants have the resources and experience necessary for multi-disciplinary problems and futures research. Moreover, because of their expertise in data acquisition, storage and selection and in identifying wants and recognising needs, they are well qualified to do problem solving and trouble shooting. In other words, they have all the makings of commercial think tanks. There are some useful lessons to be learned here from American experience where concerns like A.D. Little and Booz, Allen & Hamilton, are widening the scope of their consultancy services and tending to specialise in unstructured problems where established techniques cannot be normally applied, or where the complexity of the problem calls for a very significant research element. It is in this field that the think tank approach is likely to be particularly successful and the future may see the formation of many new think tanks based on management consultants where the problems tackled would be far removed from budgetary control, communications, formal organisations, etc.

Where the new scientific based management consultants can make their most useful contribution is in their ability to communicate, to tell managements what is happening outside those areas of knowledge which directly affect them but which have a big potential of usefulness. More and more industry is looking to the science oriented management consultants to help them find their way through the maze of the new technologies. Take for instance, Stanford Ovshinsky's threshold and memory devices (ovionic switches) which imitate a function of the human brain by permitting electronic devices to adapt their behaviour automatically to suit varying demands on them. This invention, dismissed at one time by some of the big electronic corporations in America as unworkable, has not yet been taken up on any sizeable commercial scale although it holds out great promise of revolutionising the vast electronic based industries. Since 1946, when the computer was first developed, the memory capacity has increased 1000 times, but Dr Herman Kahn of the Hudson Institute believes that by the year 2000 the computer will have improved 100 billion to 100 trillion times (whatever that means) 'to transcend' man in thinking, painting, writing poetry and every way. And in 'sex' by reproducing and improving themselves. It is devices like ovionic switches that will help to make possible this astronomical improvement.

It is in dealing with such complicated problems that the science oriented management consultant is in a privileged position to try and give management a somewhat similar type of assistance as that given by the think tanks to the United States Government in helping it to grapple with problems of national security. Just as organisations like the Hudson Institute are looking for possible futures, trying to find alternatives and new choices, so the new breed of management consultant is taking a long cool look at industry and commerce and trying to apply the analytic methods of Rand and the Institute for Defense Analyses: seeing if new management science approaches such as linear programming and simulations can make possible better planning and control or help in the evaluation of variables.

The best known of the American contract researchers are Booz-Allen Applied Research, Bjorksten Research Laboratories, Houston Research Institute and Arthur D. Little Inc., all of which offer somewhat similar service to the not-for-profit research institutes and like the latter a fairly high percentage of their work is carried out for government and state agencies, an exception being Bjorksten which does only 5–10 per cent research under contract with government. Although there is now a substantial cutback in US Government spending on outside research, this is being made good by the increased support given to these companies by industry, and by their increasing diversification, the new emphasis being in techno-economic work, such as systems analyses.

What is surprising about the pattern of non-government work is that it is the technically strong companies who give the most support, turning to the contract research companies for information in highly specialised areas of research outside their normal fields of interest which, if pursued within the company, would call for a heavy investment in staff and facilities.

For example, a chemical company troubled with an air pollution problem might want to know the biological effects of increasing atmospheric carbon dioxide or of the possible reduction in oxygen on the growth of plants and animals, the biological effects of increasing atmospheric nitrogen oxides, etc. Such work, if undertaken in the firm's own laboratories, would place a great strain on available resources and prove a difficult and expensive exercise. Apart from the rather obvious laboratory bench and field work required to establish the effect of pollution on the environment, management science can, by a systems approach, do a great deal more. It can analyse all those factors known to or likely to contribute towards pollution, going back to the basic raw materials and design of plant, the installation of recovery units and the training of staff to recognise and appreciate the importance of pollution as a real threat to society. The problem is not tackled piecemeal, but it is tackled in its entirety so that the report, when it is issued, does not merely tell the client the extent of the damage caused by waste gases and by-products but how to stop or at least reduce their output.

As in the case of the not-for-profit institutes there is a high degree of specialisation with these for-profit research companies. For example, Bjorksten Research Laboratories has achieved great success in the development of new materials, such as foamed aluminium, vinyl sizing for glass fibres and metal coated glass fibres for high strength composites.

Houston Research Institute, a wholly owned subsidiary of Space Craft Inc., is primarily engaged in the development and application of advanced technology for process industries and related government agencies and many of its activities are keyed to fast growing Houston industrial areas. This Institute has achieved notable success in developing process innovations in the local synthetic rubber and petroleum industries and was one of the first to perfect direct digital control systems for refinery processing plant.

Houston Institute has always taken a lead in the development and application of advanced data acquisition and computerised control systems and most of its military contracts with NASA and the USAF have been concerned with specialised systems and installations.

Booz-Allen Applied Research founded in 1955 is a fast growing organisation with outstanding research capabilities being exceptionally strong in techno-economic areas largely because of the powerful influence of the parent firm, Booz, Allen and Hamilton, one of the largest and oldest management consulting companies in the world. In line with practically all of the American research institutes, it does a great deal of work for government agencies, being particularly forward in adapting new technologies and techniques to military problem requirements. Its Research Office at Kansas City works closely with the US Army's Institute of Combined Arms and Support in designing war games capable of evaluating operational doctrine, organisation, structure and material requirements for the Army's CDC Program. A continuing project has been to develop and update a comprehensive automated information system for use in quickly determining basic army organisation and material factors required for specific military operations. A recently completed study involved determination of what capabilities existing military installations could provide nearby towns and cities in the event of civil disasters. Another program involved development of a series of mission scenarios for use in computer simulation of helicopter combat and support missions. The data provided by this exercise will make available to the army valuable performance requirements for future helicopter transports.

Booz-Allen Applied Research also excells in applying facility design planning skills, particularly where complex instrumentation is required, to a number of problem areas in both the military service and industry. For example one such study has been the establishment of criteria for construction of a Land Gear Dynamic Test Facility for the US Air Force Flight Dynamics Laboratory. Space sciences research has, since the earliest days of America's space program, received a great deal of attention and Booz-Allen scientists and engineers have, among many other projects, provided systems reliability and thermal systems engineering for the NASA–Goddard Orbiting Astronomical Observatory spacecraft and conducted studies of some fifty experiments designed to measure geophysical phenomena from an orbital state. The company has a very broad platform of research and during the last few years has been specially prominent in the fields of air and water pollution control, engine reliability prediction and remote area power generation. Booz-Allen Applied Research is fortunate in having at hand Foster D. Snell, a research company subsidiary particularly strong in industrial chemistry, biology, engineering and associated skills. Snell provides clients with services in all phases of chemical and biological research and testing, including conception, evaluation and development of new or improved products and processes.

One of the most interesting of the profit-making research establishments is Arthur D. Little which occupies a unique position among the for-profit think tanks. Apart from being the oldest—it was found in 1886—it is also the largest contract research company ranking alongside IITRI, Battelle and Stanford and is a bit of an odd man out in being owned by its retirement fund with the profits divided among senior employees. Where ADL scores over its competitors is in planning worldwide marketing of products and services. A few year ago it took on a major planning effort for a group of American chemical fertiliser manufacturers, the work including an analysis of basic raw material supplies and a comparative evaluation of the major chemical processes used in fertiliser production. Long range planning and diversification is a speciality of ADL. In a project carried out for North American Aviation Inc., the company in collaboration with NAA and the Harvard Economic Research Project developed a 90 sector input–output forecasting model of the US economy for projections through 1980. Forecast results included personal consumption expenditures, capital spending and inventories; Government spending, exports and imports are forecast independently and provided as inputs. On the government side ADL is a major contractor and its work for the Department of Defense has led to the development of new and improved defence systems. For the Department, ADL has explored the origins of innovations in weapons systems and analysed the management environment in which they were produced.

A.D. Little is also heavily involved in chemical engineering and typical of the projects carried out in this field was work done for the Kuwait National Petroleum Company in preparing the project description and the design construction contract for one of the world's largest and most modern refineries.

Here A. D. Little served as liaison between KNPC and the contractors, establishing reporting systems for planning and control, recommending organisational changes necessary for KNPC to adjust to rapid growth and helping to carry through the work.

This contract research company also does a great deal of work centred round urban, regional and national economic development, formulating policy for government and industry and taking care of the management of research and development in specific fields. For example, the Corps of Engineers commissioned ADL to develop 'Projective Economic Studies of New England' forecasting growth in 1980 and beyond, in population and income, the nature of regional industry and business and other factors. Here the primary purpose of the exercise was to learn how human dynamics might affect water demand, but the facts and figures of ADL's survey were made available to New England's business leaders as aids to their own long range planning.

In the commercial field ADL is interested in developing computer programmes for inventory control in retail stores. In pilot tests carried out in some American cities, 30 per cent more sales were realised on about the same total investment in stock when the programme was used to signal when and how much stock to order. Additional programmes have been developed to cover both fashion and staple control, to govern daily activities and weekly ordering, and to guide store management in setting inventory policy to meet changes in their competitive and economic environment.

ADL's research based activities have resulted in a large number of innovations, some extremely profitable, for example, instant breakfast foods, missile fuels, hot drink paper cups and low temperature cryostats, nylon fishing lines and atomic fallout filters. The company has always been to the forefront in the physical sciences with particular emphasis on new synthetic materials, such as new high temperature resistant polymers for which the aerospace research programme shows increasing interest.

It is in the realm of uncertainty in research management that A. D. Little Inc. is proving particularly helpful to industry in its search for new products or product lines, in other words, in making R & D commercially productive. Very often it is not that company research is dragging its feet but that management environment is generally unfavourable towards the adoption of the new ideas it produces. This is where a company like

ADL with its vast experience and science management is able to make substantial contributions by helping its client to help itself!

British Think Tanks

One of the most interesting and promising of the British contract and development companies that merits the term think tank is Cambridge Consultants Ltd., a small and unconventional organisation with headquarters in an old mill at St. Ives, 20 minutes car drive from Cambridge University. With a staff of 50, mainly chemical, mechanical and electronic engineers and led by Tim Eiloart, a Cambridge chemical engineer, this small think tank is well placed to tackle assignments in wide engineering fields.

Cambridge Consultants is proving particularly useful to British industry in four main fields of consultancy work:

1 By helping companies whose R & D is overextended to solve specific problems in areas outside those normally covered by the company. For example, while modern techniques have made it possible to produce carpets at great speed choice of pattern is severely limited. If traditional Axminster patterns are wanted, the traditional axminster loom has to be used and it may be possible to insert only 10 rows of pile per minute. Cambridge Consultants, by using a combination of piezo-electric, fluid logic and pneumatic techniques were able to develop a method of producing fully patterned carpet 60 times faster than the methods in common use in the industry.

Cambridge Consultants analysed the problem and saw in it a means of applying new ideas in electronics and mechanical engineering which the carpet manufacturers would not be expected to apply being too heavily involved in the technologies of manufacture.

2 To assist a commercial concern to introduce new products or product lines, e.g. in 1967 Audits of Great Britain wanted a TV meter to record the times a set is switched on to each programme and thus provided minute-by-minute audience measurement. Each record has to be accurate to half a minute or better and the record be capable of being automatically read by computer. An instrument was developed using digital recording on heat sensitive paper. It is of interest here to note that the first unit was successfully designed, built and demonstrated 16 weeks

after the job was taken on and the final instrument helped AGB to gain the contract for the UK audience measurement service.

3 To collaborate with industry in exploring new development areas. One such example was a system for handling packaged goods of random weight that was capable of complete sorting by weight, pricing and stamping. Cambridge Consultants developed here the channelising electronic system for this installation.

4 To undertake general consultancy work in techno-economic fields, such as examining diversification opportunities for a company whose market is stagnant, mobilising resources for product innovation, research and consumer product planning, applied research and problem solving, outlining new recruitment and training policies, science management and market studies. Cambridge Consultants is becoming increasingly involved in this type of work. The company was employed to estimate the use and to give the potential demand for silos of various types in the UK with special reference to applicability and costs. It looked closely into the market for glass fibre reinforced plastics, reviewed the opportunities which existed in new container devices with special reference to desirable innovations.

In contrast to American think tanks, many of which are comfortably cushioned by fat government contracts, Cambridge Consultants does only a small amount of work for government departments (although naturally it would like to do more) and it relies almost entirely on the contacts it has with industry. The main emphasis in all the projects undertaken at St. Ives is creativity and the best evidence of this is the large number of new projects and patents that come out of the workshops every month.

There is certainly nothing lush about this think tank. Overheads are pared to a minimum, workshops and offices consist only of the bare essentials, just four whitewashed walls and the necessary woodwork. There are few floor coverings and no comfortable furniture—the visitor is given a kitchen chair to sit on! However, lighting and heating are adequate and there is a heavy investment in machine tools and high quality electronic test equipment. If the premises do not impress the visitor the enthusiasm of the staff certainly does, and it is an enthusiasm that is shared not only by the project leader whose responsibility it is to direct the team doing the work, but by the model maker who builds the first prototype and the part timer—usually a student from one of the universities working at St. Ives during his vacation.

The atmosphere is deceptively casual, more typical of the University campus than an industrial R & D establishment and there is a complete lack of the usual establishment ideas of management. The staff work with and not for the executive directors. Everyone, from the teenager at reception who also operates the telephone exchange, to the Chairman himself, seems to enjoy working at St. Ives and creative flair, upon which the company depends for its existence, is kept alive by what Tim Eiloart calls 'creative drive'; he breaks it down into originality, serenity, enthusiasm, curiosity, resourcefulness, opportunism, stamina, flexibility, dedication and energy.

The mechanics of problem solving in a think tank such as Cambridge Consultants are worth examining. First of all, the problem is defined and analysed to see if it is one problem or several ones, if it can be broken down into sub-problems, if it is allied to other problems in the same field, some of which may have been solved, who else had a similar problem and what did he do about it? Possible, unlikely and impossible approaches to a solution are examined, theories considered. The team allocated to the task is given its points of contact, encouraged to discuss it with other members of the staff, to listen to any idea no matter how nonsensical to brainstorm in groups—especially drinking groups; to sleep on the problem, run, walk and play with it; to wander through stimulating environments such as junk yards, science museums, fair grounds, Woolworths, farmyards and city streets; to browse among scientific, technical and trade journals (particularly old ones) and even comics.

Sometimes the clue to important discoveries lies buried in long and turgid papers published by obscure societies. Mendel's great work on the hereditary behaviour of certain hybrid characters lay buried in a paper he addressed to the obscure Society of Natural History of Brno in 1865 which no one bothered to read until 1900 when Mendel's laws were rediscovered by the German biologist C. Correns and the Dutchman H. de Vries. The sudden idea, the flash of blinding and revealing thought, the significance of the accident, any one of these can point the way to a new path for the researchers to follow. It was a happy accident in 1940 when some catalysed polyester resin was spilt over several layers of glass fibre and produced the first GRP material, later to be widely applied in boat building, industrialised building and to found new industries.

Poincaré pointed out that the sudden appearance of a flash of inspiration invariably follows on days of unfruitful work and the team leader has to be alert to this. Frequently the ideal solution to a problem may be identified, only to find that it is impossible to implement because of cost or complexity, etc. and the researchers have, therefore, to do something quite different, to sidestep the problem itself and approach it by a new and unexplored route. Cambridge Consultants stress the importance of the inter-disciplinary approach Rand has found so necessary in systems analysis work. For example a problem in mechanical engineering may be worth discussing with an economist, and even a student in theology might have something to contribute.

To the conventional R & D establishment in industry all this may seem rather untidy and unprofessional, but experience has demonstrated quite convincingly that these apparently random actions if pursued with enthusiasm and drive are capable of producing some astonishing results. So far Cambridge Consultants have been chiefly concerned with engineering projects, the emphasis being on electronics and mechanical science, but as new disciplines are added they will undoubtedly penetrate into new areas, particularly the biosciences.

Many of the projects undertaken at Cambridge Consultants are small ones but everyone has an important 'piece of the action', everyone is made to feel that his contribution is a significant one, everyone is involved in the work; the engineers, draughtsmen, model makers and the odd job man are not just nameless faces in a big and often soulless organisation.

Although Europe's and the UK's largest consulting group, P.A. Management Consultants Ltd. has never called itself a think tank, nonetheless, some of the problems it is now being asked to solve might well come within the range of a think tank. Moreover, with over 1000 professionally qualified consultants highly skilled in a number of disciplines in both the hard and soft sciences and experience in just about every sector of industry, commerce and public administration, plus its established links with universities and contract research establishments the right talents are at hand to cope with most situations. Because of its background, management consultants such as P.A. are most likely to achieve initial success in the field of economic planning where there is a requirement to make a fundamental reappraisal of the economics of regions and countries as the basis of future development. At the moment P.A. is carrying out a study for the Isle of Man Government that will form the basis of a long term plan for the island's future and this will cover every facet: tourism, industry and agricultural and the retirement community.

P.A. is particularly at home with fundamental policy studies for commercial firms which set out to answer the question 'What is our business and what should it be?' As a result of the multi-disciplinary approach P.A. has had some notable success in what might be termed 'transplant' knowhow, i.e. giving tired and sick businesses a new and vigorous personality and going far beyond just curing defects for clients which is what a management consultancy is supposed to do. An insurance company whose growth was below par developed into a successful finance house, an obsolescent dockyard into a profitable hovercraft business, an overcentralised international communications company into a number of autonomous regional units each with the ability to develop new local business.

On the technological side, an example of the way in which P.A.'s consulting and technical strengths combine in a 'think tank' mode is illustrated in a contract with one of the major electronic instrumentation companies. Here P.A. is retained to continuously evaluate past and current scientific and techno-logical research and to propose new or improved measurement techniques. Several important new advances in measurement science have already been evolved by combining various scientific disciplines with the management consultant's experi-ence of production processes and markets.

The author believes that the future of the commercial type of think tank may well lie with the management consultant and this type of organisation is likely to become increasingly involved in technological development and research because so many of the problems facing industry today, even those misleadingly concerned with economics, have their roots deep in technology.

7 THE ADVISORY NON-PROFIT CORPORATIONS

No one quite knows how many advisory think tanks have grown up round America's postwar defence and aerospace programmes but the number is an impressive one, and some say as many as 350. Each of the three military services has several large establishments which have in turn spawned many smaller units; the Defense Department has the massive Institute for Defense Analysis (IDA) and most of the Federal agencies concerned with missile, electronic, atomic and aerospace technologies have their own advisory corporations most of them specialising in systems analysis. While the US Navy has the Center for Naval Analyses (CNA) as a division of the Franklin Institute in Philadelphia, and the Army its independent Research Analysis Corporation (RAC), the US Air Force has the Rand Corporation, the most famous of all think tanks. Although the Air Force sponsors a number of other quite important non-profit corporations, including Analytic Services Inc. (ANSER), The System Development Corporation (SDC), Aerospace and MITRE, there is no doubt that Rand (the name was coined by an elision of the phrase R & D standing for research and development) is by far the most important, enjoying a much greater degree of freedom of action than is found in the other establishments.

While American Government civilian agencies have, on many occasions, evinced an interest in think tanks only HUD with its new Institute for Urban Affairs and possibly OEO with its institute at the University of Wisconsin have made any positive move in creating them.

How and why did the public service non-profit corporations come into existence? What purpose do they serve?

Echoing Rand's Charter it could perhaps be said that they

were formed 'to further and promote scientific, educational and charitable purposes all for the public welfare of the United States of America'; or in the words of the Hudson Institute 'to provide for government agencies and other clients the kind of assistance the President of the United States receives before making a decision; nobody tells the President what to do, but advisors do present alternative solutions and bases for choice.'

Although not in any way disbelieving these objectives, it is a fact that these institutions were not founded purely for altruistic reasons. The lessons which the Government of the United States learned during the Second World War, through the workings of emergency organisations such as the Manhattan District and the Office of Scientific Research and Development, convinced those in power that if the USA were to remain ahead in weaponry it was necessary to have available for consultation and problem solving an élite corps of civilian scientists to do the new thinking about military forces and weapons and about strategy and policy planning. In other words to provide decision makers in government with the kind of independent top ranking advice which the military and the civilian agencies were not fully qualified to give because they lacked the time and the skill to analyse the situations that confronted them!

Although Project Rand was designed primarily to provide the US Air Force with the research facilities which it lacked, the idea of recruiting a civilian organisation to help it out was not altogether popular in some quarters and the inclusion of a high proportion of social scientists in the original Rand team was not at first acceptable to General Le May, Air Force Deputy Chief of Staff, although he was willing to be convinced that social science might be able to play an important part in Rand's new approach to research.

Later the pattern of Rand's recruitment of professional staff was widely adopted by other advisory corporations. Rand was not born overnight. The idea of a kind of procurement agency for buying brains was tossed about by the Top Brass at the Pentagon for some time and gradually crystallised into forming some kind of private organisation made up of the best civilian brains that could assist the services in planning for future weapons development. As Bruce L. Smith points out in his book on *The Rand Corporation*, the Douglas Aircraft Company which first housed and generally looked after the original Rank chick when it was hatched was very enthusiastic about the whole conception of a think tank designed to help the US Air Force.

However, later on some high ranking USAF officers thought that Rand did too good a job and were opposed to the idea of an outside body having the kind of freedom which the corporation enjoyed.

The Rand objective as spelt out by the USAF in 1946 was 'a programme of study and research on the broad subject of inter-continental warfare other than surface' which allowed researchers a surprisingly large amount of scope. And, from the beginning, Rand scientists made their own rules, worked only on those projects they thought worthwhile and important and not necessarily on what the USAF considered useful. Moreover, Rand has always decided what completed research to show to the USAF and what to keep to itself. It is no wonder, therefore, that some sensitive toes in the hierarchy should be trodden on.

R. D. Specht in *A Personal View of Rand History*, a paper he presented on 23 October 1958, to the Operations Research Society of America said that:

> 'Douglas assigned some of its best men to form the nucleus of the new organisation and went out of its way to make the new group at home. Still, Douglas found itself foster parent to an odd and, I am sure, often irritating offspring.'

However, later the presence of Rand at Douglas became a business liability and so the Rand Corporation came into being as an entirely independent non-profit advisory corporation.

The idea of forming the independent non-profit advisory corporation, an organisation quite unique in American history, was a brilliant one. As it had no stocks and no stockholders and, with none of its assets benefiting any individual, there could never be any criticism of profit-seeking and corruption in high places. Moreover as the advisory corporation is governed by its Board of Trustees, representing the public interest, there could be no whisper of nepotism.

After a somewhat shaky start, the Rand Corporation proved an outstanding success and more than justified the high hopes of its military parents. Rand is unique among the think tanks. Fortunately it is not in any way worried about finance and enjoys sound institutional funding and researchers have not to worry too much about pleasing their sponsors. It enjoys, if not complete freedom, at least a very high degree of independence and within reasonable limits staff are encouraged to pursue their own lines of study and enquiry no matter where they lead. Rand has earned an international and impressive reputation that is the envy of every other think tank.

While the inter-disciplinary approach to problem solving may not be a Rand invention, it was at Santa Monica that this unorthodox and yet effective method of tackling a complex problem was highly developed and produced such surprisingly good results. The idea that economists, political scientists, engineers, mathematicians and physicists should work cheek by jowl on a major technical project for 6 or 12 months seems on the face of it a trifle odd, particularly if the study covers territories unfamiliar to some of the researchers. Yet by learning each others' language and concepts and discussing common interests considerable progress is made in lightening the dark areas of knowledge.

Although Rand's work is still primarily concerned with problems having national security implications, a new emphasis is being given to non-military studies, some of which are paid for by the Foundations, such as Ford. The broad areas of research at Rand fall fairly neatly into four general categories:

1 International relations.
2 Planning and procurement: support and operations of military forces including study of strategic and tactical forces, command and control of systems and logistics management.
3 Problems of modern society: health care, education, transportation, communication, racial discrimination, poverty, housing, environmental pollution, public order and more generally the function of government in providing public services.
4 Basic and applied research in science, technology and methodology: seeking fundamental advances in such fields as mathematics, computer sciences, economics, physics and the biosciences and applying new knowledge to specific problems in these and other fields.

The great progress made during the last few years in long range forecasting and planning owes much to the pioneer work carried out in think tanks, such as Rand, and much of the organisation's high reputation stems from its almost uncanny success in predicting major happenings. It was a Rand researcher, F. H. Clauser, who on 2 May 1946 wrote a paper entitled 'Preliminary design of an experimental world circulating spaceship' in which he set forth arguments supporting the theory that a primitive spaceship could be launched as early as 1952 and predicted that by 1957 the Russians would have launched such a craft. Other Rand scientists engaged on this study pinpointed the Russian Sputnik to within a fortnight of its actual launching date.

It was Rand's report 'Inquiry into the feasibility of weather reconnaissance from a satellite vehicle' in 1951 which made possible the launching and ultimate success of the American weather satellite programme in 1960. In the nuclear field Rand has also been extremely active and since the early days of thermonuclear development the Corporation has been thinking ahead of all its implications and analysing situations that might arise 10 or 20 years in the future. Rand physicists have not only played a vital role in helping to understand the effects of nuclear weapons but provided much of the data needed for the design of nuclear test programmes and also devised ways of disarming incoming missiles. A Rand report made as early as 1948 on an analysis of the temperature, pressure and density of the atmosphere extending to about 10,000 miles altitude formed the basis of many essential calculations, including re-entry of satellites and missiles and was, in fact, the standard reference in this field for several years.

The Hudson Institute, formed by the Rand scholar Herman Kahn, author of *On Thermonuclear War* is a small but powerful non-profit advisory body engaged on policy research. Although patterned after Rand, which Hudson thinks is too technical and too obsessed with the idea of nuclear deterrents, this Institute has more doves than hawks on its staff of analysts and is less concerned with nuclear strategy, its primary objective being to understand the workings of war so as to be able to control it. However, along with Rand and the other 'in-the-family' advisory corporations, Hudson is obliged to accept (although not without question) the official US Government's strategy of deterrence. Unlike Rand, which owes allegiance to the USAF, which pays for most of its work, the Hudson Institute owes allegiance to no single agency although the bulk of its work is commissioned by the government: Kahn asserts that whereas Rand functions as a client's 'loyal' opposition, Hudson serves as the 'disloyal' opposition, taking nothing for granted and questioning everything.

In complete contrast, The Institute for Defense Analysis (IDA) is concerned only with defence matters and within its rather rigid and highly professional framework sets out to provide an independent and objective source of analyses, evaluations and advice for the United States Government.

Whereas Hudson struggles along on a meagre budget of $1·2 million and looks to the charitable foundations and industry for increasing support, IDA has a budget of $14 million, all from government sources, and Rand's budget exceeds $22 million.

In comparison with other defence non-profit corporations, Rand is somewhat unique in the degree of independence it enjoys. Unlike the other advisory corporations sponsored directly by one of the services, Rand is not controlled by the US Air Force but has a contractual relationship with it. This difference is brought out in the articles of incorporation which sets out that upon dissolution of the Corporation all of Rand's assets will go to the Ford Foundation, whereas with the other service sponsored advisory Corporations, all assets, on dissolution of the establishment, go to the US Government.

Rand's independence is reflected in its dealing with sponsors and Rand itself admits that they would enjoy Rand more, but value it less, if Rand were always to agree with them. Research and results are never constrained to support particular policies or plans, and the detached quality and objectivity of the corporation's work is well understood and appreciated at various points in government. Indeed US Government agencies are so impressed with the worldwide reputation and performance of Rand that they tend to use the Rand yardstick when assessing the usefulness and potential of any existing non-profit institution and frequently recommend that the Rand blueprint should be used when laying down the foundations of a new one. And Rand itself has had a direct hand in forming several splinter groups concerned with highly specialised operations which Rand Trustees thought were outside the research remit of the corporation. For example, The Systems Development Corporation (SDC) was created by Rand to help in the designing and programming of the first computerised air defence system (SAGE) (for Semi-Automatic Ground Environment) and when the systems engineering and training aspects of the operation got too big, Rand felt it was time for it to become independent. Analytic Services Incorporated (ANSER) was spun off by Rand when it was felt that the work involved was out of keeping with the research objectives which the Corporation always tried to follow. (It is interesting to note here that SDC became a for-profit taxpaying corporation in 1969 although the not-for-profit organisation, which has no connection with the management and operations of the new corporation, continues as System Development Foundation.)

Unlike the independent contract research institutes which the author refers to as the think tank laboratories, the advisory corporations may not have laboratories in the usual sense and the term research can sometimes be misleading when applied to their activities, the Hudson Institute disclaiming that it does 'scientific' work in the generally accepted sense or attempts to discover new basic knowledge or theories, being consumers of science rather than producers. Hudson's seven modern buildings on the 21 acre site at Croton-on-Hudson, some 30 miles from New York City, contains only a very active reference library, conference rooms of various sizes, a dining-hall and space for private study offices and support facilities. There are no scientific establishments, experimental workshops or even a computer and the only tools of science likely to be found are slide rules, and of course blackboards. In one of the conference rooms there may be a seminar taking place about the wider implications of Herman Kahn's and Tony Wiener's book *The Year 2000: A Framework for Speculation*, with particular reference to planning in the fields of education and urban development. In another room a group is discussing Vietnam and particularly hamlet development and possible economic development ideas in South Vietnam. In one of the corridors an ecologist, he might be Ronald Dagon formerly with the New York Botanical Gardens, is talking to an engineer from one of the big aircraft companies about the Choco Project, one of the most ambitious and far-reaching studies of a non-warlike nature ever undertaken by the Hudson Institute.

The casual and homely atmosphere at Hudson contrasts markedly with that of most advisory corporations where security guards check up on visitors and where few outsiders actually penetrate beyond reception. While there are no Battelle Memorial type laboratories at Rand's Santa Monica headquarters, there are computers and a great deal of electronic equipment deemed necessary for the type of research that Rand carries out. At IDA one of the most important divisions of the corporation is the computer group which has a staff of 10 professionals and 13 supporting personnel, primarily pro-grammers and computer operators. Generally where work in the physical sciences is deemed necessary for a research project this is contracted out to one of the research institutes or university.

Much of the pioneer work on titanium, previously unusable

in flight structures, was brought to industrial technology in the early years of the Rand Corporation by Rand-supported experimental research at Battelle Memorial Institute. Rand works closely with universities, research institutes, medical centres and private individuals on some of its projects. In its work on stroke detection Rand scientists collaborated closely with local physicians to create the tools and procedures that may one day permit a diagnostic screening centre to be set up to detect and give advance warning of incipient strokes so that currently available remedial procedures may be used to prevent a stroke from occurring.

In another bio-engineering field, open heart surgery, Rand has been working closely with the University of California, Los Angeles, on developing optimisation criteria for evaluating extra-corporeal blood oxygenation systems. There is a very close line between the universities and the advisory corporations and it is recognised that the success of many studies depends largely on the degree of cooperation existing between the two types of organisations.

The Institute for Defense Analysis was founded by the major universities in the USA who were asked by the government to sponsor a Rand-like advisory group that could work closely on research contracts for the military departments. IDA's initial function was to administer a research contract in support of the Weapons System Evaluation Group which works for the Joint Chiefs.

A research group at IDA known as JASON has been set up that is made up entirely of outstanding university scientists who spend an important part of their time on studying complex technical problems and feeding into the IDA network new information about scientific discoveries and research which might usefully be exploited in the interest of national programmes. Twice or more during the year these university dons gather at IDA headquarters for 3-day weekend meetings designed primarily to keep them abreast of current scientific problems of interest to the Government.

IDA works on a number of Pentagon research contracts, each division assigned to a specific military department. For example, the Research and Engineering Support Division works almost exclusively for the Office of the Director of Development Research and Engineering, while the Economics and Political Studies Division works primarily for Civil Defense and for the Assistant Secretaries in charge of Systems Analysis and International Security Administration. As Dr

Stephen Enke, head of Economics and Special Studies at TEMPO points out in his paper on 'Think tanks for better government', IDA has never really become the 'Rand of OSD (Office of the Secretary of Defense) and it has sometimes addressed subjects unduly limited in scope. Moreover the IDA trustees have sometimes seen IDA as not much more than an administrator of independent research contracts for different Pentagon customers.'

Hudson's research staff and consultants are drawn from university faculties, government service, scientific and engineering research, law and journalism. Basically Hudson's major objectives are to stimulate and stretch the imagination; clarify, define, name and argue major issues and to design and study alternative policy combinations and policy making contexts. Alongside these are various subsidiary objectives including the design and study of various aids and tools useful to the policy maker, long range planner and analyst. A great deal of the work carried out by the advisory corporations is concerned with systems analysis, a form of study applied to the broader and more complex national problems, such as an appraisal of new weapon systems where the more tightly controlled operations research or analysis cannot be applied.

Some of the government sponsored think tanks, for example Center for Naval Analysis (CNA) seem to do little else than systems analysis and have made their most important contributions in this field.

The Research Analysis Corporation (RAC) is also heavily involved in this type of work for its principal customer the US Army. Other groups funded by the military, such as MITRE, are primarily systems analysis contractors. It is important to bear in mind that some of these military think tanks were created originally to one kind of job, in many instances to give 'systems engineering support' and it was never envisaged that they would become permanent organisations.

However, the US military departments have come to lean very heavily on their advisory bodies and it is most unlikely that they would ever want to get rid of them unless budgetary cuts made this imperative. It is appreciated that only think tanks have available the highly qualified (and extremely well paid) civilian scientists and engineers capable of tackling the urgent and complex problems which crowd in. The civilian government agencies could certainly profit from having at hand advisers of the calibre of Rand or IDA, but according to Dr Enke they appear to resent any interference from outside sources.

Systems analysis is not only applied to military problems but has wide application. For example, in 1959, Rand was asked by the Ford Foundation to assess the applicability of systems analysis to the study of elementary and secondary education in the United States. As a result of this preliminary exploration, the study was continued under the joint sponsorship of The Ford Foundation and Rand. It is recorded that suggestions in the report formed the basis of action in a number of school districts throughout the country.

With most of the advisory corporations a high percentage of the research projects are classified and as a result most of the publications that are issued come under a tight security ban. At Rand every effort is made to see that a high proportion of the specialised knowledge accumulated by the staff is made available to the public. During 15 years the Corporation has distributed over a million copies of about 7000 Rand publications. Included are 150,000 copies of about 2700 technical papers, prepared for presentation at scientific meetings or for publication in professional journals and 300,000 copies of about 70 books, issued by commercial publishers and university presses. At Hudson, while most of the research papers are not available for outside distribution, a number of books and reports are issued for general release.

The Advisory Corporations: Some Typical Fields of Interest

IDA

Tactical systems	Optics technology
Strategic systems	Information sciences
Sea warfare	Energy conversion
Re-entry physics	Radar propagation
Weapons effects	Laser technology
Missile defence	Advanced propulsion
Space technology	Counter insurgency
Advanced	Microwave justice technology

RAND

Ramjets	Aircraft design
Rocket engines	Air traffic
High energy fuels	High energy radiation
Analog and digital computers	Nuclear proliferation
Radar detection	Strategic missile systems
Atmospheric physics	Strategic bombers
Metal fatigue	Nuclear options study
Air defence	Strategic arms control
Nuclear propulsion	

Rand Non-Military Projects

Studies of the earth's magnetic field in order to improve predictions of the strength and patterns of the magnetic field as it affects the radiation belt.

Research on electromagnetic compatibility dealing with present and future electromagnetic environments, including techniques for measuring and analysing frequence spectrum usage, saturation, interference and frequency allocation and assignment.

Image enhancement to increase the effectiveness with which information can be transferred to man.

Study of computer based systems for filming, retrieving and analysing large masses of data that arise in cancer research.

Linguistic research on developing computer techniques for solving grammar and semantics problems, on applying these techniques to investigate the structure of English and Russian and on applying them to problems of information retrieval and mechanical translation.

Long range planning and study of Rand-developed 'Delphi' procedures particularly as applied to technological forecasting and use in areas of education, health and transportation.

Evaluating manpower training programmes.

Analysis of the nature and causes of racial disparities in income, directed as a widespread confusion between poverty and racial discrimination.

Study of the economy of the metropolitan area of New York.

Some Recent Hudson Research Projects

Political, strategic, tactical and technological factors that may affect the threat or use of force during the period 1968–1978.

Technological aspects in information transfer and its role in bargaining and war.

Stability and tranquillity among older nations.

Vietnam.

Alternative political and strategic environments for Air Force systems in the period 1975–1985.

International peace-keeping.

Anti-poverty studies.

Choco Valley Study, Ministry of Public Works. Republic of Colombia.

War termination.

Analytic summary of US national security policy issues.

Post-attack social organisation.

New York city.

Inter-American Development Bank.

8 THE ADVISORY PROFIT-MAKING CORPORATIONS

Although most of the military think tanks work on specific tasks set by their Pentagon customers, both Rand and Hudson have much broader terms of reference and are not so concerned with systems analysis as general policy research, being particularly adept in dealing with highly complex situations where objectives cannot be defined very easily and where it is not possible to provide neat solutions to set problems. Recommendations when they are made are usually in the form of alternatives and may even contradict one another. With the profit-making corporations problems are usually well defined and tasks need to be completed to deadlines set by the customers. However, the bulk of their work is still with military operations. For example SDC which in 1969 billed some $60 millions in contracts, has three divisions concerned solely with military work: air operations, space and range and command support operations. Military billings at SDC total $50 million and in 1969 were up by 12·9 per cent.

While studies carried out by non-profit think tanks sometimes end up as hardware produced by other contractors, e.g. Rand's researchers in the realm of missile and satellite technology helped immensely in the large scale development of the first Atlas ICBM, most of them finish as fairly static reports, many of them classified, which are essentially analyses, surveys and recommendations for decision makers in government, state and industry.

One of the leaders in this field is the System Development Corporation, the most experienced and one of the largest of the profit-making think tanks specialising in information technology and system sciences. It has more than 3000 employees and is strategically sited in eight major business areas in the United States. SDC is a favourite with the Pentagon because of its very practical approach to problems and is used extensively by the military to cope with the realities of defence in new environments. It provides advanced studies and simulation, systems analysis and engineering, software system design, implementation and testing, system exercising and training and operational support.

SDC is also heavily involved in aerospace research and has applied its skills in information processing, systems engineering, operations research and behavioural sciences to a variety of problems associated with space operations. These have included advanced feasibility studies, software specifications for range and satellite support data systems, telemetry computer program development and integration, orbit determination, real-time control of space network operations and development of space oriented programming languages and compilers. However, SDC does a great deal of business in non-military fields and its public systems and commercial systems divisions are kept at high pressure applying the Corporation's unique experience in time-sharing and the systems sciences to the commercial market. The commercial systems division is now serving a number of clients throughout North America through the development and installation of software products and applications packages, as well as through an entirely new service, the SDC Datacenter, which provides the user with a multi-purpose and flexible information management system.

Current contracts require SDC to use a total of 200 computers and its research and technology laboratory provides an array of display scopes and teletypes to perform computer based research and development projects. Its continuing programme of research and development is aimed at advancing the art of computer technology, at increasing the corporation's competence in problem solving and at learning more about national and commercial problem areas.

Another big performer in information technology and systems sciences is the $57 million Planning Research Corporation. A great deal of its work like that of SDC's centres round the analysis, design and implementation of computer software systems. This includes systems that operate in real time, computer programs for scientific use, proprietary commercial programs, commercial customs, applications and military applications. In all the US military departments where it operates this advisory corporation plays a highly important role: for the army an improvement and extension of resource estimating procedures for an automatic data processing system; expansions to a system for computer control of artillery and for the implementation of a large management information system. Projects for the Navy include a message processing system designed for automatic input, storage, distribution and transmission of messages. Important work for Headquarters, United States Air Force, consists of design and pre-implementation planning for a new generation computer system. For ground, sea and air strategic commands third generation computers are now playing a vital part and their programming calls for a broad knowledge of systems analysis and computer systems which only an organisation such as this is able to provide. The Corporation can answer the questions: 'Is the project technically and economically feasible? What is the optimal way to accomplish it?' Any combination of 50 disciplines may then be applied to carry the project forward to completion. The Planning Research Corporation is also one of America's largest sources of professional services for airport and airline managements, providing systems analysis for airport master plans, simulation of terminal and air space traffic, design engineering and supervision of all aspects of airport construction—buildings, runways, roads and intra-airport transit systems—computer flight planning and computer documentation of cargo.

The profit-making advisory corporations also carry out economic research from feasibility and market studies to urban and international development studies, traffic and transport. They not only work directly for government but act as sub-contractors for the Federal Agency or military's main contractors responsible for the hardware and they also do an increasing amount of work for industry. The Planning Research Corporation derives 46·7 per cent of its very large revenue from commercial and overseas projects; 13·8 per cent from state and local governments; 4·8 per cent from civilian agencies of the Federal Government and 34·7 per cent from military agencies of the Federal Government or their contractors.

A different type of organisation is TRW's System Group, one of six operating units of the mighty TRW Inc., which employs 80,000 people in 300 worldwide locations and has an annual sales volume of approximately $1·5 billion. The Group's advisory work is designed primarily to generate hardware, its systems engineering and technical direction efforts beginning with the United States' earliest ballistic missiles and going from there into all the military and space projects as well as a large number of industrial products.

The TRW's Systems Group, which came into being in 1953 to do the system's engineering for the US Air Force, employs 17,000 men and women of which 7000 are graduate. Its main fields of interest include engineering, physical sciences, life sciences, behavioural sciences, computer sciences, management sciences and the humanities and it can be regarded as the think tank for the manufacturing divisions of the company.

Another entirely different profit-making think tank is TEMPO (Technical Military Planning Operation and now also Technical Management Planning Operation) which was established by the General Electric Company of America in 1956 to do some of the advanced thinking in defence systems which the military required at that time.

While this Center for Advanced Studies acts in an advisory capacity as a think tank for GEC top management (20 per cent of its work is taken up in this way) its main function is as an adviser to the US and foreign governments and those sections of industry not competing in any way with GEC. Exceptionally strong in systems analyses, which is hardly surprising as several of the top analysts are ex-Rand scholars, it is also foremost in technological forecasting. Today TEMPO, although its largest client is the United States Government, is very much involved in management planning in industry, not only with the giant General Electric Corporation, but outside. TEMPO is entirely self-supporting on its fee income which ranges from $7 to $10 million a year. A great deal of this Center's work is overseas. Some of its staff are on loan to the World Bank to study future power and transportation requirements for India and to make suggestions about a suitable level of investment for the World Bank. Much of the Center's work is future oriented, dealing with development beyond the next 5 years and especially with problems of transition. Areas of current concern include:

> Regional economic development.
> Technology and management planning.
> Computer and communications systems.
> Problems of urbanisation and industrialisation.

In all its work TEMPO stresses the fact that while it cannot establish goals or make decisions, it can help in relating an organisation, whether it's a government department or a private company, a city or a country, to its changing environment, and assist in helping it to define its objectives and analyse alternative technical and economic approaches to the fulfilment of goals. The result of TEMPO's work is highly relevant information in usable form providing a better understanding of options, their requirements and their implications. This makes it possible to select among wider alternatives and to make sounder decisions. TEMPO stresses the fact that its success in problem solving starts off with the client himself identifying the problem and realising that the Center's unique experience may help in finding a solution.

Then there is the tiny IR & T (International Research and Technology Corporation) with a professional staff of 23. It does not, like the giant TRW Group, exist to generate hardware or other business for its corporate affiliate EG & G Inc., an important Massachusetts Company, but it is organised as a diversified, inter-disciplinary group dedicated to finding ways of coping with social and environmental problems arising from the use and abuse of technology. Although it has not been in existence many years this think tank has been responsible for a number of major projects, in arms control and disarmament; nuclear safeguards designed to prevent the diversion of nuclear materials from the civilian nuclear industry for military, criminal or other destructive uses; space technology and its potential industrial applications; transportation technology, especially in relation to its impact on community development and environmental side effects; heat systems technology, environmental pollution, urban problems, conservation of scarce resources, technological forecasting and information retrieval methods. The corporation has undertaken projects in all these fields for national and international agencies, private institutions and other corporations.

One rather frightening project which IT & T carried out under subcontract with Stanford Research Institute, was a survey of the ways in which organised groups of criminals, e.g. the Mafia or political extremists might acquire nuclear explosives and use them for blackmail, sabotage, terrorism or other purposes. Particular attention was paid to a study of the types of information, people and facilities required for small organisations to fabricate and test several different types of nuclear explosives. Backing this up was a survey of historical acts of violence that might bear on the credibility of non-national nuclear threats.

IR & T undertakes a number of company sponsored projects providing opportunities and facilities for the corporation's researchers to pursue their own pet ideas and here they have achieved great success: the open cycle air engine, super-conducting magnetic suspension systems for high speed ground transportation systems, a method for producing radioactive isotopes in space, the study of alternative fuels for Rankine cycle engines and the development of a new technique to facilitate planning and decision making. The last named promises to assume considerable importance both in government and industry. Nicknamed SYNERGI (Systematic Numerical Evaluation and Rating by Group Iteration) it is designed to reduce the influence of unrecognised subjective attitudes or values upon major policy decisions. It consists of a detailed outline of all objectives to be weighed during resolution of a specific problem, a list of the available methods or solutions under consideration, a presentation of the factual base upon which the decision must rest and a procedure for repeated discussion and a voting on each of the component elements of the decision. Originally derived from the Rand Delphi method, the SYNERGI technique is designed to improve the reliability of decisions involving uncertainties of the present, as well as of the future. It has the added advantage of speed; the judgement feed back and refinement processes are combined in a single session with the aid of an electronic device developed expressly for this purpose.

What is particularly interesting about the work of these advisory corporations is the increasing emphasis given to the behavioural sciences. For example, one of the most important subsidiaries of the Planning Research Corporation is the Behavior Science Corporation formed to apply behavioural sciences to business, education and government problems. A typical study carried out for airlines included public opinion surveys, assessments of airline services and evaluations of world markets. While some of these activities might be considered to be outside the scope of what a think tank might be expected to do, the Corporation believes that because of its inter-disciplinary approach it is able to bring to this type of evaluation new skills, techniques and an expertise that the airline industry would not find in the conventional Market Research Company. The new science of psychographics (i.e. determining the psychological characteristics of people as these characteristics relate to people's behaviour as consumers) has an important bearing on product selection and preference and the Planning Research Corporation is finding an increasing awareness of its importance in a number of commercial projects where an unusually high degree of advertising assessment of the mass media is required.

9 THE PHILOSOPHICAL THINK TANKS

As opposed to the advisory corporations working for government which might be described as the hawks in the think tank business, there are the doves, the non-profit institutions engaged in philosophical enquiry and educational work. They have nothing to do with planning, their work is not sponsored by any Federal agency and they undertake no contract work for industry. Most of them have close ties with the universities or are actually part of a university. For example, the Center for Strategic and International Studies is a self-financing affiliate of Georgetown University. The Foreign Policy Research Institute forms part of the University of Pennsylvania, the Center for Research on Conflict Resolution is lined up with the University of Michigan and the Institute for Advanced Study relies heavily on a fortunate symbiosis with Princeton University.

Harvard University Program on Technology and Society is an integral part of Harvard University (established by a grant from IBM in 1964). Hoover Institution of War, Revolution and Peace, grown from a small documentary collection on the First World War (founded 50 years ago) to a million volume research library, is an independent institution within the framework of Stanford University. Apart from the many university connected institutions, there are a number which have no ties with any seat of learning. For example, the Center for the Study of Democratic Institutions stands alone and so does the unconventional Western Behavioral Sciences Institute.

How are these places financed? With the exception of the Center for the Study of Democratic Institutions, which relies for its funds on private subscriptions from members, the majority are dependent on help from their universities, the various foundations, such as Ford, Rockefeller and Mellon, etc., and private sponsors. Their budgets vary in size from $2 million plus for the Institute for Advanced Study to less than a quarter of a million dollars for the Center for Strategic and International Studies.

With some of the smaller institutes fund-raising presents great problems: it is often easier to find funds for small scattered research projects than for sustained programmes of research and in both instances they suffer from not being able to announce spectacular discoveries like a new vaccine or a new planet. At the Center for Research on Conflict Resolution at the University of Michigan, primarily concerned with insights into the balance of power, the analysis of conflict situations such as racial conflict and the study of social conditions conducive to conflict, much of the labour of the Center's directors and staff goes into fund-raising.

The kind of problems which the philosophical think tanks try to bring into focus, although none would claim to solve them, deal with the great crisis issues facing the world today, such as the causes of war, racial conflict, poverty, crime, health and the effects of the new technologies on society, industry and the environment and their impact on man himself. Many of these programmes of research are long term calling for analysis and case studies spread over many months or years. For example, Harvard University Program on Technology and Society is a continuing programme devoted to the effect of technology change on four major areas:

1 The life of the individual.
2 Social and individual values.
3 The political organisation of society.
4 The structure and process of social institutions.

A few of these think tanks are 'do-gooders' and seek to advance humanitarian causes. The Western Behavioral Sciences Institute is one of the last named. It breaks with the scientific tradition of 'arms-length' involvement and seeks to invent approaches that sacrifice neither scientific objectivity nor the ardour of full commitment to a responsibility for social change. A primary purpose behind the founding of WBSI in 1959 was the conviction that it was becoming increasingly difficult in academic institutions to carry out truly innovative research and to nurture ideas that lead to fundamental shifts in thinking. This Institute enlists the cooperation of the foremost thinkers in the field, bringing them together in work sessions and study conferences to produce overviews of the state of knowledge. In a way this part of the program is modelled after the Neurosciences Research Project at MIT which has developed techniques to bring greater coherence into our understanding of how the brain works. The efforts of Harvard University Program on Technology and Society to understand and to assess the threats that technology poses, its negative impact on people's jobs, on their material and spiritual wellbeing, on human institutions and on the physical environment are likely to produce some far-reaching results and their advanced thinking may help to change the pattern of future government behaviour.

In spite of their small budget, modern establishments and small numbers of staff, these philosophical think tanks exert a powerful effect on public affairs and are often able to influence governmental decisions. This they are able to achieve by means of their publications which reach a broad intellectual public as well as lectures and seminars which keep them in touch with the people who really count in government, industry, commerce and the professions. As the members who constitute the Faculty of these think tanks are drawn not only from the academic world, but the military services, industry, commerce and sometimes the church and as they are all acknowledged experts in their particular fields, their reports are accepted by government officials, leaders of industry and informed people abroad as authoritative, closely reasoned and completely impartial. Because they are aloof from the centres of power and have the freedom to stand back from problems and examine them objectively, they are often able to generate useful new ideas and to suggest new methods of approach. Moreover, by providing reliable, up-to-date information on vital topics they are in the position very often to brief the policy makers. Whatever is issued by these organisations is always taken seriously and read with interest by newspaper editors, TV commentators, government and community leaders, although they sometimes disagree quite violently with what they read. Staff members and associates of these think tanks frequently participate in, and address, conferences and programmes sponsored by universities, governmental agencies, communication media and research institutes. Sometimes they organise conventions, such as Pacem in Terris II which was held by the Center for the Study of Democratic Institutions, in Geneva in 1967, and attended by more than 300 distinguished persons from 70 nations.

The Center for Strategic and International Studies looks

upon its primary work as the preparation of reports, each one limited to 100 pages and prepared under the auspices of a expert panel which guides the staff work, defines the scope of the study and releases the report. Over the past two years the Center has published six special reports and plans to continue the series at the rate of three or four a year.

Reports already published include:

Soviet sea power.
Nato after Czechoslovakia.
The Gulf: implications of British withdrawal.
The Soviet military technological challenge.
Economic impact of Vietnam War.

Studies now being developed for Special Reports include:

The US role in the Western Pacific.
Outlook on the Indian Ocean for the 1970's.
Trends in Canada's foreign policy.
The Suez Canal opened or closed.
Brazil and the key issues in its possible future.

Although broadly speaking the institutions given over to philosophical enquiry have one thing in common—the desire to carry out a broad programme of non-partisan research on major policy issues, followed by discussion and publication—they differ markedly in their choice of subjects and their approach to the work.

Some, such as the Center for Strategic and International Studies keep fairly rigidly to international affairs, monitoring the horizon in search of signs of new problems, research gaps and shifts in priorities and with listening posts in many foreign capitals. Others like the Foreign Policy Research Institute of the University of Pennsylvania not only look at the international scene but study the influence of technology on future political order in various countries. Although all these establishments are strictly non-partisan, they are identified, rightly or wrongly in the minds of the public, with belonging to certain political groups. In the early days of the Fund for the Republic, which is the legal entity of the center for the Study of Democratic Institutions and preceded it by several years, it came under bitter attack by Senator Joseph R. McCarthy during his witch hunt for Communists in high places. The fact that the Fund was established to defend and advance the principles of the Declaration of Independence, the American Constitution and the Bill of Rights was never really believed either by the Right or even the Left. In its time both the Fund and later the Center have been accused of being un-American, favouring communism, encouraging negro extremists and student activists and generally trying to interfere in America's domestic and foreign policies.

But Marxists and Trotskyists have also criticised the Center because of its impartiality and clear-sighted analyses of major issues of policy, the fact that it tries to give the pros as well as the cons when solutions are sought to problems.

Most of these think tanks place a heavy reliance on inter-disciplinary research and analysis. The small staff at the Center for Strategic and International Studies is made up of a distinguished ex-admiral, retired military men, historians, social scientist, lawyers, a commercial analyst, librarian, journalist and specialists in foreign affairs—twenty in all.

The Center's Research Council which coordinates and integrates the work with that of international scholars and experts uses the services of economists, historians, political scientists, physical scientists, former Ambassadors and experts in foreign affairs. Project are first studied by Center Panels and Study Groups to define their scope and dimensions and then it is decided what international experts should be brought in so as to help in the collection and analysis of the necessary data and the final analysis and report. The Center for the Study of Democratic Institutions in Santa Barbara has a Dean who is an eminent sociologist and twenty two fellows made up of a professor of the humanities, journalists (which seem to predominate), authors, philosophers, two Episcopal Bishops, newspaper ex-editors, educationalists and a Nobel Prize winning research chemist.

These twenty three people gather daily around a conference table for recorded dialogues on basic issues of the day and these can range from a discussion about multi-national corporations, conglomerate mergers, the aftermath of civil war in Nigeria, the possibility of a Russian/Chinese war, to philanthropic foundations, the control of science and technology and the future of the city. The Center looks upon itself as an organised group, rather than a collection of individuals, which is free of any obligation except to join in the effort to understand the subjects they have selected to study. Its President, Robert M. Hutchings calls it 'an intellectual community' and then goes on to say that 'its talk is oriented to action. It talks about what ought to be done.'

In contrast the Institute for Advanced Study at Princeton, New Jersey, might be considered to be a very passive body. Although partaking of the character both of a university and of a research institute, it differs in significant ways from both. It is unlike a university in its small size, its academic membership not exceeding 150. Then again it has no scheduled courses of instruction, no commitment that all branches of learning be represented in its Faculty and members. It is unlike a research institute because its purposes are broader, it supports many separate fields of study, maintains no laboratories and welcomes temporary members. Founded in 1930 by a gift of Mr Louis Bamberger and his sister, Mrs Felix Field, the Institute for Advanced Study has for its primary purpose:

'. . . the pursuit of advanced learning and exploration in fields of pure science and high scholarship to the utmost degree that the facilities of the institution and the ability of the faculty and students will permit. Its first professors were eminent in pure mathematics and mathematical physics, archaeology, history and economics and its three schools are devoted to mathematics, natural sciences and historical studies. In the natural sciences theoretical physicists, astro-physicists and astronomers tend to predominate.'

IO THE FUTURIST THINK TANKS

At the end of the Second World War military planners in the United States were faced with the task of developing weapons systems that would not be rendered obsolete before they came into use and they looked to the scientist to provide them with some kind of workable formula that would take long range forecasting out of the realms of guesswork. What the Pentagon wanted was the ability to predict military situations and the balance of power 10, 20 and 30 years ahead and to be given some idea of the trend of the technological developments— the new inventions, discoveries and innovations that might arise to alter the whole thinking of weaponry design.

While it was soon realised that there was no magic formula available that would give the military strategists a precise idea of the demands of military operations in the future world environments or the new technologies likely to alter the whole pattern of future weapons systems, techniques could be developed capable of rationalising prediction and taking it away from the old crystal ball gazing of the fortune teller. What arose was not one method or system but a complex process of systems producing what Eric Jantsch (Consultant to the OECD) calls 'a probalistic assessment, on a relatively high confidence level.'

However, it was not only the military that was anxious to plan ahead with a reasonable chance of success, but the civilian agencies of government, industry, commerce and the professions soon began to realise that in the face of fast changing technologies, social changes and social needs, long range planning was not possible without taking all these factors into account and to do this involved forecasting events a decade or so ahead. For example, agencies on the civil side involved in planning new towns had to try and forecast developments in all the areas affecting the life of the community—urban development, transportation, pollution of the environment, communications, medical services, water supplies and power requirements—5, 10 and 20 years ahead. In planning the new city of Milton Keynes in the heart of the Buckinghamshire countryside, the planners have had to work against a backcloth of scientifically prepared forecasts of urban life in Britain 20 years ahead. For example, in their interim report published in 1968 the planners placed great emphasis on social planning and the need to design sophisticated social monitoring systems and social development systems for the new city. They looked forward to an increasingly affluent society in which there was a very high level of car ownership and a big demand for house ownership (half of the houses in Milton Keynes will be sold). Jobs will be created to absorb available labour and sited so as to even out traffic flow; health and educational services provided on a scale to meet the maximum, not minimum population growth and distribution of goods and essential services planned on the same generous lines.

In every walk of life there is a growing consciousness of the importance of long range forecasting as an integral part of long range planning, and the general concern shown to develop scientifically based forecasting techniques stems from the assumption held by the planners that the future is not destined and that it can be changed or guided by knowledge gained today and action taken today. The alternative is a grim one; to sit back and watch haphazard, uncontrolled technological and social changes accelerate at such a rate that there is a complete breakdown of society. The so-called normative method of forecasting appears to have a great deal in its favour; the goal is decided upon at some distant point in time and all man's efforts directed towards attaining that goal. In other words, he sets out deliberately to take the necessary measures to control his destiny, or rather other people's destiny! To many people, however, this Galbraithian approach has menacing social implications as it tends to restrict freedom of choice and, of course, ultimately the freedom of the individual.

Dr Simon Ramo, vice-chairman of TRW Incorporated, says, 'We must try to predict and prepare for the impact of technology. The world is so dangerously complicated—and accelerating technological change and lagging social progress are so mismatched—that we cannot afford to wait and react to unexpected events after they occur.' In his book *Cure for Chaos: Fresh Solutions to Social Problems through Systems Approach*, Dr Ramo describes how this sort of approach can best be applied to industrial, social and governmental problems, in this order of complexity.

Although it is appreciated that long range forecasting is still an uncertain business, it can, if it is based on careful judgement, provide the manufacturer with some useful guidelines:

1 By suggesting alternative courses of action.
2 By indicating where dangers may be lurking if certain actions are taken.
3 By defining the scope of reasonable expectations in a fast changing world.

According to a McGraw-Hill Survey about 90 per cent of American firms did forward planning in 1966 compared with only 20 per cent in 1947, and added to this is the fact that 600 of the major American companies currently spend 1 per cent of their R & D budget on long range forecasting as an aid to management.

Typical of the kind of long range forecasting and planning service available in American industry is the Maptek service offered by Quantum Science Corporation and successfully used for several years by major corporations. It is based on major extension of input–output methodology and clearly reveals the many interrelationships between the different parts of the US economy and specific products. The results of this market research effort include market forecasts and other data on all parts of the economy, including a wide range of subjects, forecasts technological trends, present and future competitive environment and optimum corporate strategies to be employed in the projected industrial environment.

One of the biggest of the American firms in the prediction business is TRW Incorporated, a very big corporation providing a wide range of products and services to space, defence, automotive, electronics and selected industrial and commercial markets. It employs 80,000 people including 2 per cent of all the physicists in the USA and has an annual sales volume of approximately $1·5 billion. Its systems engineering and technical direction efforts, involving long range forecasting which Dr Ramo, its vice-chairman, calls 'scientific anticipation of change', began with America's earliest ballistic missiles, Thor, Atlas and Titan I and were continued through the Titan II and Minuteman I and II programmes. Today TRW is providing similar support to Minuteman III, America's most advanced ICBM.

In British industry there is a growing interest in the systems approach, but only the monolithic corporations, such as ICI, Shell, BP, Unilever, etc. and the more progressive of the medium sized firms in the growth industries are yet convinced that the high cost and complexity of modern American methods justify the results.

The Systems Research Division at British Telecommunications Research Ltd., Plessey Telecommunications Group, is one of the British companies that believes in the systems approach as the only logical method of defining the complete problem, setting goals, measuring progress towards them, gathering all available data, examining alternatives and then coming up with the best balanced solution. In a paper on 'Needs research' published in *Futures*, September 1969, Mr R. I. Hart, Head of the Systems Research Division explains that the Plessey team first aims at studying the user (in the telecommunications field) and trying to assess his needs and follows this by studying 'the state of the art of technology in terms of materials, devices and techniques in an attempt to see which of these might be embodied in new communication systems which could satisfy the need. These two activities lead to a specification for a systems research programme which will lead to a new product appearing on the market.'

Commercial firms are also trying to look into the medium and longer range future, and the Inter-Bank Research Organisation, established in October 1968 by the London Clearing Banks has formed its own 'think tank' to plan banking as far ahead as the year 2000. Its multi-disciplinary team of about 20 specialists in electronics, computing, systems analysis, economics, statistics, accountancy, law and government as well as banking is studying a number of projects, most of them concerned in some way with the future implications of the computer and how automation, standardisation and simplification of banking practice are likely to affect future relations with the customer, with the government and with foreign investors.

On the perimeters of British industry there are a number of consultants, agencies and special service companies offering long range forecasting and planning and, of course, all kinds of societies, associations and other bodies are involved in a study of social problems calling for long range planning. Most of the universities are very much concerned with new forecasting techniques and their application to social problems. For example the Design Laboratory of the University of Manchester Institute of Science and Technology is heavily involved in futures research, so also is the University of Aston's Design and Innovation Group, the University of Bradford Management Centre and Strathclyde's Centre for Industrial Innovation.

There are in the United States 400 think tanks engaged on long range forecasting and no one can hazard a guess of the number of government establishments, universities and colleges doing similar work. There is little doubt that America is far ahead of the rest of the world when it comes to prediction, both as regards the number of organisations who carry it out and the reliance placed on the results by governmental and business planners. However, there are in Europe a number of institutions engaged in 'futurology'. France has always taken a very keen interest in forecasting techniques and prominent among the organisations is the Bureau d'Information et de Previsions Economiques (BIPE) founded in 1958 and owned jointly by the French Government and 50 of the most important industrial concerns in the Republic. There is also the non-profit Societé d'Etudes et de Documentation Économiques Industrielles et Sociales (SEDEIS) which was at one time funded by the Ford Foundation. 1970 was the tenth anniversary of the founding of the International Futucibles Committee in France and to mark the occasion a House of Futucibles (Maison de Futucibles) is to open in Paris.

In West Germany there is the non-profit-making institution Studiengruppe fuer Systemforschung financed by the Federal Government and working almost exclusively for government and the newly created Hoste Institute catering mainly for long range forecasting as applied to industry and in the words of its founder, Professor Holste, to form 'a systematic coordinating centre in planning for industry'.

In Vienna there is an Institute for Questions of the Future (Institut für Zukunftsfragen) directed by Robert Jungck. In Sweden the military and civil planners have been particularly successful in integrating both medium and long range forecasting with planning. It is interesting to note that the Royal Swedish Academy of Engineering Societies, an independent institution with government support, is proposing to set up the first Forecasting Institute in the country. This will be financed partly by the central government and partly by charitable foundations, industry and private organisations.

Its main functions will be the development and distribution of methodology and theory of long range forecasting; to act as a clearing house for information; initiation and management of integrated futures studies and educational work as applied to different levels in the community. Creation of such a body should serve a most useful purpose not only in making available to any organisation, government department, local authority or industrial concern the services of an efficiently run independent long range forecasting unit, but to act as a clearing house for information. In Denmark there are two closely linked organisations doing research on futures: the Academy for Research on Futures and the Society for Research on Futures. Finance is supplied mainly by private foundations although some support is given by the government.

In Belgium, Italy, Switzerland there are also institutions engaged in long range planning and, of course, there are the international organisations, such as the European Economic Community, Brussels; Euratom Economic Commission for Europe (ECE) in Geneva which prepares economic forecasts; Food and Agriculture Organisation (FAO) whose work touches the fringe of forecasting; Organisation for Economic Cooperation and Development (OECD) and the European Coal and Steel Community (CECA) which carries out long range forecasting as applied to iron and steel; the Union Internationale de Telecommunications (UIT) which does planning up to the year 2000; United Nations (UN) and the United Nations Educational, Scientific and Cultural Organisation (UNESCO) forecasting. This rather sketchy survey does not, naturally, take into account the many consultants and agencies of various kinds who offer a planning service to business and, since Erich Jantsch's exhaustive survey of technological forecasting in OECD countries in 1967, there has been a general awakening of interest in this new discipline.

Israel is also becoming live to the practical advantages of futures research and an Association for Futurology and Philosophy of Technics and Science has recently been formed. Its published aims are to carry out research in futurology, philosophy of technics and philosophy of sciences and to publish and disseminate information and knowledge in these fields in Israel and abroad.

In the USSR increasing emphasis is being given to the science of science problems and technological forecasting and at the great centres of science—Moscow, Leningrad, Novosibirsk and Kiev (where there is held a highly successful annual symposium on futurology) teams of eminent Soviet scientists are engaged on this work. It is significant that during the last 5 years the pace of research in this field has quickened very appreciably, increasing attention being given to the application of mathematical methods and computers to technological forecasting in line with current American practice.

Japan's Economic Planning Agency is one of the most successful in the world and it is, of course, freely acknowledged that this country's planning has produced results that have amazed its trade competitors with its almost uncanny accuracy. Unlike the methods used at American centres, such as Stanford, the Japanese approach to long range planning is largely intuitive, often pragmatic techniques developed as the result of experience and highly specialised study are preferred to scientific methods.

In the United Kingdom long range planning is carried out by the Ministry of Defence, Ministry of Technology and other Government Departments as well as the nationalised industries. The Central Electricity Generating Board is particularly concerned with technological forecasting. Although techno-logical forecasting is carried out in Britain's universities as part of sundry research programmes and the large industrial companies do a great deal of work in long range planning which takes in most of the recognised American techniques, there is no Institute of the Future, and attempts to form a national body to study futures methodologies and to offer a long range planning service to industry have been abortive. So far there is no real appreciation in Britain of the need for such a body and futurology is still viewed with considerable misgivings many quite influential people, in and out of govern-ment, looking upon it as little more than American gimmickry.

Long range forecasting as a scientifically controlled discipline is an American invention. If one cares to go back to 1937 there is a US Federal Government publication entitled *Technological Trends and National Policy* which attempted to peer into the future but missed almost every important inven-tion and discovery of the next decade. However, it can be said that technological forecasting really got under way after the Second World War when it became an essential part of the long range planning of nuclear weapons. One of the earliest and most ambitious long range forecasting services was made available by TEMPO, General Electric's Center for Advanced Studies in Santa Barbara, California, which was set up in 1956 to help the defence department in analysing nuclear test data and weapons systems and to assist in long range planning. Since 1963 this organisation has functioned as a semi-autonomous self-sustaining think tank within the General Electric Company in which it acts in an advisory capacity for top management and with about 80 per cent of its work contracted out to the US Government and industry. The speciality of TEMPO is the application of strategic techniques to business.

Another pioneer of long range planning was Stanford Research Institute which in 1958 launched a research programme to provide research based planning information to corporate executives on a regular, continuing basis. The SRI Long Range Planning Programme became a means of monitoring changes in technical, economic, political and social fields and interpreting these changes in terms of their impacts on the business environment. Through the mechanism of multi-sponsorship the Programme enabled a number of companies to share in the results of a research effort that no single company could afford. The central function of LRPP is to provide a series of reports—about 40 per year—on changes that will have major impacts on industry. Each report—authored or co-authored by a specialist in the field—contains an analysis and outlook on an individual subject, with emphasis on the implications for various categories of industry. The wide range of subjects includes micro-encapsulation, corporate earnings, cryogenics, anti-trust policies, reinforced plastics, internationalisation of industry, nuclear power, as well as consumer values and pleasure travel.

Battelle Memorial is also foremost in this field and since 1950, when it contributed towards President Truman's Poley Report which set out to project the natural resources needs of the United States in 1975, it has been making forecasts for government and industry. The Geneva branch of Battelle is particularly active in technological forecasting as applied to future Common Market countries and international organisations, such as CECA. The Columbus Institute in Ohio is under contract with US Federal agencies, e.g. NASA, and has many industrial sponsors. Technological forecasting plays a prominent part in Battelle's general research and development work. The advisory corporations such as the Rand Corporation and the Hudson Institute have always been deeply involved in long range planning and much of the progress made in methodology is due to research work carried out by these organisations on systems analysis. Rand is specially identified with work on new forecasting techniques, such as learning curves, gaming, model building and the Delphi method. The last named is really a refined form of brainstorming. In the words of Rand the Delphi technique 'involves using a systematic exercise, conducted in several iterations, with carefully controlled feedback between rounds to reduce the biasing effects of dominant individuals and group pressures'. Today the Delphi method is widely applied in forecasting and opens up new and fascinating avenues of research in what is now known as 'opinion technology'.

There are a large number of research and management companies, consultants and agencies which are committed to long range forecasting as part of the corporate planning carried out for industry, and practically all of these are American. There are firms like A. D. Little, Abt Associates, International Research and Technology or IR & T, Corplan Associates (a profit-making splinter group from the Illinois Institute of Technology or IITRI), The Planning Research Corporation, Samson/Quantum Science Corporation and management consultants like McKinsey & Co., Booz, Allen & Hamilton (which has acquired a small British subsidiary, Business Operations Research), A. T. Kearney also with interests in the UK in the form of Norcross and Partners Ltd. All these concerns and many more provide industry with a medium and long range forecasting service.

With some companies, such as A. D. Little, industry is offered a package deal on a subscription basis (somewhat similar to Stanford Institute) or technological forecasting is done for a group of manufacturers—what is termed multi-client research. The alternative is long range forecasting tailored to suit a specific product or manufacturer. With many of these organisations there is a high degree of specialisation, some being primarily concerned with long range planning in research and development such as Corplan Associates and A. D. Little, while others, particularly the management consultant firms, are mainly preoccupied with marketing strategies.

Quite apart from these institutions and companies doing long range forecasting as one of their many disciplines, there are two futurist think tanks, Resources for the Future and the newly created Institute for the Future, both American and concerned solely with research into the future although in different ways. Resources for the Future, is a non-profit, tax exempt corporation established in 1952 with the cooperation of the Ford Foundation. Its purpose is to advance the development, conservation and use of natural resources through programmes of research and education. Generally speaking Resources for the Future specialises in problem oriented research and recent projects included a study of possible alternatives to the internal combustion engine; quality of the environment; land use and management and regional and urban studies, all of which involve looking into the future and examining long range possibilities. For instance, in the case of the internal combustion engine radical new engine designs were examined and new types of fuel considered.

The Institute for the Future is an entirely different type of organisation and, in fact, it is the only one of its kind in the United States (if not the world). It is dedicated exclusively to systematic and comprehensive studies of the long range future and does no other work. IFF's organisers say that the Institute has broader objectives than the established think tanks, longer range horizons and no dominant clients. In effect the Institute for the Future devotes its basic effort to socio-economic problems. An early piece of research for example carried out by the IFF was a study of 'Forecasts of some technological and scientific developments and their social consequences', the scenarios covering the technological world of 1985, 2000 and 2025. This research is particularly interesting not only on the active content of the study but because it was used as a test case for the Delphi method which in the past has proved particularly valuable for long range forecasting of expected technological and sociological developments.

Forecasting Techniques

There is nothing really novel about forecasting, for there have been seers, prophets, astrologers and soothsayers since the dawn of history. In commerce it has long come under the term of 'business judgement' and the success of a firm has often depended on its ability to plan ahead, using long term estimates of acceptable accuracy as useful guidelines.

The job of estimating or forecasting sales, production, etc., is usually delegated to a member of the staff who has a particular flair for this kind of work. Sometimes his predictions are close to the target and at others he is well out in his reckoning. While the one man effort can still produce reasonable forecasts when applied to fairly simple situations, it tends to break down when the problem becomes complex and when the impact of new technological and sociological changes has to be taken into consideration. To cater for the complex situations, technological forecasting has been evolved as a new scientific discipline in which a number of skills may be employed and special techniques developed to cater for different types of problems. While a great deal of mumbo jumbo has been written about technological forecasting and many exaggerated claims made for its accuracy, there is no doubt that it can improve business judgement and so prove a valuable aid to management.

There are two basic approaches to forecasting, one starting from the past and present and working forward step by step, identifying the opportunities that are presented, towards a goal some years ahead; the other, starting from a point out in time and working backwards, locating and describing the obstacles or threats that have to be overcome in order to reach the goal. Within these frameworks all kinds of techniques have been worked out by researchers, choice of method being largely influenced by the kind of forecast that is to be made.

The purpose of the exercise may not be entirely obvious, although objectives may be more clearly defined as the study progresses. For example, a firm may want to find out what anticipating actions are called for or when decisions will have to be taken to reach certain goals, or it might want to know the direction in which its R & D programme should be redirected in order to reach a certain product objective 20 years ahead. Some types of forecasting are relatively simple. A firm in the plastics business, for example, might want to find out the volume of polyethylene that would be required for packaging in the UK in 1980. By canvassing expert opinions on the company's sales staff, plus opinions of the main users of polyethylene film, the packaging machinery manufacturers and the other producers of film and studying the growth of the business over the last 5 years it should be possible to come up with an acceptable forecast. However, such a forecast might well be grossly inaccurate if it did not take into account the impact of new plastics discoveries which could challenge the position of polyethylene film in packaging, or the effect of new sociological attitudes towards the increasing use of a type of film that is virtually imperishable.

Broadly speaking, forecasting techniques tend to fall into three broad categories:

1 *Time-series analyses* covering demographic/sociological forecasting, parameter analyses and expert opinion. These are designed to tell when things can be made to happen or when

things will happen that will affect certain situations. The best known of these techniques is parameter analyses which sets out to determine trends and to use this information to forecast future performance, and expert opinion or the Delphi method developed by the Rand Corporation. The latter represents probably the great advance in forecasting as it evaluates group judgement for policy formulation. All kinds of refinements are possible with Delphi but essential it consists of first choosing a number of experts in the particular subject to be studied and then sending them a series of questionnaires through the post in which they are asked to use their judgement in answering the question. The replies, which may vary quite considerably, are then returned to the participants in the exercise who are asked to reconsider their answers in the light of the group opinion, giving reasons for any variations. The third round robin contains the revised estimates and the reasons why the participants differ from the majority is then sent out for reassessment. The final result produces a consensus of opinion and while it does not claim to be precise it does define the scope of reasonable expectation in a specific field.

2 *Systems analyses* developed out of earlier operations research strives to be more comprehensive in its scope, taking into account all the relevant factors which have any bearing on the problem, which is usually a complex one. Rand which, more than anyone else in the business, has helped to develop systems analyses and apply it to new weapon systems describes it as referring 'to the complex problems of choice among alternative future systems, where degrees of freedom and the uncertainties are large, where the difficulty lies as much in deciding what ought to be done as in how to do it.' The more clearly defined the 'system' to be examined, the simpler it is to find clear cut solutions. For example, in a business study decision making is primarily concerned with the profit motive and this can be measured in terms of money. Moreover the firm operates in areas which are clearly defined and the conditions governing actions are thoroughly understood by all those concerned in the analyses. On the other hand, problems in the political and military fields seldom have a single objective like profit. Indeed, the objectives may not even be clearly defined or they could even be disputed and the perimeters of the problem areas may be unknown. There may be systems within systems.

One of the tools which Rand has found particularly useful in highly complex situations is that of operational gaming or simulation by groups of people—quasi-experimentation. This it is claimed lays the right kind of emphasis on clarity in problem formulation. It allows the inclusion of qualitative factors and provides a means by which scholars in several different fields can work together, applying their intuition and advice to common problems. Rand games have dealt, for example, with hypothetical offence and defence force structures for the United States and the Soviet Union over the next decade, with contingencies in the cold war, and with the design and effectiveness of military assistance programmes. The essential feature of all games is personal involvement of the players. Games are designed for specific purposes, e.g. instructional, training or communications, the first being the most important as they focus attention on decision making and problem solving and are readily applicable to a great variety of situations facing government, industry, commerce, education and the professions. Some games are like charades, except that they are not played off the cuff but follow a scenario prepared beforehand by those organising the game and designed specifically to present certain opportunities for problem solving and decision making. The objectives or set of objectives is clearly defined. For example, a business game which Booz, Allen and Hamilton Inc., helped to develop focused on management decision making and was known as Top Management Decision Simulation.

A game known as GREMEX (Goddard Research Engineering Management Exercise) is used by NASA scientists and technicians to give experience in managing space flight projects. The most advanced games use computer simulation and are very complicated. Indeed some of them may take weeks or even months to complete. Other techniques widely used in forecasting include morphology. Quite briefly this is 'the science of form' and has much in common with the engineer's value analysis as it sets out to analyse the operation of an existing product or process, to break down its operation into steps and then to examine each step so as to find out the various ways in which it can be performed.

Morphological analyses was invented by the Swiss astronomer Fritz Zwicky who published a book on the *Morphology of Propulsive Power* in which he examined all possible kinds of jet engines. One version of Zwicky's 'morphological research' is used by General Electrics TEMPO for assessing military rocket development. Another valuable technique is scenario writing. This starts from the present and imagines the logical sequence of events towards the future, comparing them so as to identify crisis points and points of decision. Herman Kahn, the presiding genius of the Hudson Institute and author of the book *On Thinking the Unthinkable—A Study of the Problems of Thermonuclear Strategy*, is a firm advocate of scenario writing. He claims that by this method the analyst 'gets a feel for events' and is able to identify possible important decisions and alternative solutions to problems.

3 *Relevance analyses*, which has particular application to business studies, and is best characterised by the pattern technique, a relevance tree scheme developed by Honeywell and the rating scheme of De l'Estoile of the French Ministère des Armes.

I I   THINK TANKS AND PROBLEM
SOLVING

*The real key to successful research is to match the proper research
men with the problems to be solved. But of equal importance is the
way in which research people are motivated. Obviously the selection,
direction and motivation of technical people is all important if
management is to get what it expects from research. Creative effort
has been described as 'The imagination that looks forward, foresees,
supplies, completes plans, invents, solves, advances, originates.'
It is significant that there is not a single passive verb in this
whole list.*

DR CHARLES N. KIMBALL
MIDWEST RESEARCH INSTITUTE

Some present day problems are so complex, so difficult to
define, so inextricably mixed up with other problems and
involving such obscure interrelationships that clear cut
solutions become impossible and the most one can hope for is
some kind of rational approach to the problem that will
provide 'demonstrably good' or defensible solutions. In the
major problems of national security in America, think tanks
like Rand and the System Development Corporation have
shown that the physical aspects cannot be separated from the
international, political and economic aspects. While physical
science is competent to look at the broad spectrum of weapon
systems it is not possible to do so in isolation from their environments and context and this means taking into account a
number of outside factors relating to the affairs of nations; the
balance of power in say 10 or 20 years time; new political
thinking; changes in the political system and the effect of new
technologies on the proliferation of nuclear weapons. For

example, one highly significant new technology is the development of the gas centrifuge method of enriching uranium needed
for reactors producing electricity which provides a relatively
straightforward route to the manufacture of nuclear weapons.
Since the signing of the British/Dutch/German agreement the
centrifuge process is now a reality within the grasp of every
nation with some industrial potential so that within a few
years it is possible that nuclear weapons will no longer be
restricted to the super-powers. Japan is expected to decide in
favour of independent nuclear weapons development within
the next 5 years. India, in the face of threats from China, is
almost certain to make its own medium range nuclear missiles
and so what might seem in 1970 to be a sound defence policy
for the Far East becomes no longer tenable in the light of new
developments.

But it is not only in security matters that problems prove
difficult if not impossible to solve completely. In every field of
human endeavour a fast-changing technology is affecting the
affairs of man to such an extent that questions relating to
'how' and 'why' are quite beyond the capacity of the ordinary
institutions to find satisfactory answers. No longer can these
problems be settled by political debate; experts are needed to
detect and to analyse social events and to formulate policies
adequate to the complexity of social issues.

Experience itself is no longer adequate to tackle major
problems because of their many faceted complexities and the
fact that before any attempt can be made to solve them they
need first to be understood. To do this calls for information
and data, often a great deal of it collected from many sources,
and it all has to be studied closely, processed and analysed.
It is impossible to isolate problems from their environments,
yet if these are to be taken fully into account efforts are called
for that are often well beyond the capabilities of the policy
makers and the planners.

Narrowing down the problem to what is misleadingly called
the bare essentials does not mean that it becomes any simpler to
solve, merely that it loses its true identity. There are, in fact, no
short cuts to major problem solving and no substitute for the
serious deep thinking that is so necessary in order to understand
them. Thinking needs time, often a great deal of it, freedom to
pursue independently chosen lines of enquiry, perhaps the
mobilisation of several disciplines and skills and the use of
new intellectual tools. In government as well as in industry
administrative problems crowd out substantive matters,

decisions have often to be taken quickly without proper consideration of their consequences, situations cannot be properly analysed before they reach crisis point. This often means that major problems, really complex ones, are never solved only shelved. And this kind of situation is likely to continue until those in command, whether they are in government or industry, are given some help, and the help that is likely to be most useful is professional advice of Rand-type scholars and experts in one or more of the research institutes, such as TEMPO, Hudson and other think tanks.

Problems often seem insoluble because they are not properly understood: understanding a problem is sometimes more difficult than solving it. Some problems are misleadingly simple and invite clear cut solutions that turn out unsatisfactory because they fail to reach the core of the problem and touch only its perimeters. For example, a Middle East country might pose the problem, say to the World Bank, of how best to convert vast tracts of arid desert into productive arable land? Straightforward enough and calling for study by ecologists and other experts. But is this the real problem? Surely it lies with the country's urgent need to increase its food production: trying to make corn grow in the desert will certainly help to relieve a difficult situation, but it will not solve the problem. Once this is fully realised then the true problem can be tackled in its entirety: studies made of the country's agricultural policy, plans drawn up to increase mechanisation, provide more fertilisers, ensure more efficient farm management, better distribution of seeds, better marketing, etc. The core of the problem, i.e. how to produce more food, may be capable of solution, but how to turn a desert into a wheat belt is not the solution.

The first essential in problem solving is an appreciation of the true position, not as it appears to be, but as it really is, and such an appreciation is only possible by challenging the validity of all the so-called facts that hedge in the problem. A company plagued with labour troubles may think that the major problem facing its management is how to prevent its employees from downing tools and walking out of the factory, but they would be wrong. The major problem is not to find a formula for preventing labour disputes but to discover why they take place in the first instance. The tendency always is to look too closely at the end products of problems, particularly those affecting people, and not the beginnings. The grievances of the workers—unsatisfactory wage structure, poor working conditions, union rivalry, unsympathetic management, inadequate communications—these may be real enough and perhaps justify the withdrawal of labour, but the real ignition points which spark off the trouble and inflame every issue may be quite unknown, and perhaps have little to do with the much-vented grievances.

In solving problems of great complexity the ordinary approaches are sometimes inadequate and use has to be made of special types, methods or techniques specially developed for certain problem areas, e.g. input–output for analysing markets and determining the independence of various segments of a country's economy and systems analysis to clarify choice under conditions of great uncertainty, such as those presented by national problems.

Dealing first with input–output, this methodology is only a few years old, although the basic idea is not new. Today it is finding wide acceptance in business circles, becoming increasingly valuable as concerns such as Samson Science and its subsidiary, Quantum Science Corporation, now make available a complete component input–output service. Its tables have an application to a wide number of products and industries, particularly those in advanced technology fields, such as electronic equipment, electronic components, computer equipment, computer services and technological materials industries. As explained by Samson, the key feature of input–output is its applicability to forecasting the changes in demand caused by variations in end-markets or by technological changes in the design of a product. Therefore, input–output analysis is obviously most useful in defining the intricate interrelationships that build upon each other. They start with the component and component parts industries and then broaden out to encompass equipment market analyses and systems projections, as well as the simulation of many alternate worlds and what they will look like.

The System's Approach to Problem Solving

Systems analysis is a set of new techniques which think tanks have developed and adapted to the needs of management decision making, planning and the design of 'things', ranging, as in the case of the System Development Corporation, one of the biggest systems analysis contractors in the United States, from military weapons systems to school scheduling. Unlike operations research developed during the Second World War to solve technical problems of great complexity, systems analysis does not set out specifically to provide a quantitative answer to a problem but rather to clarify choice under conditions of great uncertainty. There is no fixed formula for systems analysis, methods or intellectual tools being chosen by the analysts to suit particular problems utilising an inter-disciplinary approach and drawing upon the social sciences, data processing, engineering and mathematics and calling in, where necessary, outside skills and expert opinions. Some of the intellectual tools used by the study groups are unusual. For example Rand has found operational gaming or simulation by groups of people—quasi-experimentation—very useful. In explaining this somewhat novel approach Rand says:

> 'The method lays particular emphasis on clarity in problem formulation. It allows the inclusion of qualitative factors. It also provides a means by which scholars in several fields can work together, applying their tuition and advice to common problems. Rand games have dealt, for example, with hypothetical offence and defence force structures for the United States and the Soviet Union over the next decade, with contingencies in the cold war and with the design and effectiveness of military assistance programmes.'

Systems analysis, which has been termed 'quantified common sense' sets out to take all the fat out of the problem and to expose its real structure. Indeed, one of its main objectives is to identify all the distinguishable elements and to determine what cause and effect relationships exist between these elements. The technique is also capable of achieving a great deal more by identifying needs and requirements before attempting to take any remedial steps to actually solve the problem. The aim of the analyst is to provide the decision maker with comparative information and selection criteria and not to usurp his authority or do his job. Gary E. Cathcart, Research Director in the Chicago office of Booz-Allen Applied Research Inc., and an authority on systems analysis says that:

> 'In practice, the decision maker generally receives the results of an analysis in one of two forms: either an optimum alternative is recommended which is backed up by supporting justification, or all possible alternatives are presented together with separate evaluations of all the factors associated with each alternative.'

The basic conception of systems analysis is the recognition that society is made up of a network of systems, systems that perform independent tasks, get support and are supported by adjacent systems.

It is interesting to note here that 3000 years ago the Egyptians were using the concept of systems planning when developing their networks of irrigation canals and storage reservoirs in the time of Rameses II and the Romans later applied the same principles when they laid out their cities and designed water systems.

The first step in systems thinking is to isolate, conceptually, the system to be studied, i.e. to describe and define its boundaries in substantial detail. In defining the process, System Development Corporation give as an example the administrative system within a larger educational system. The analysts having defined its boundaries then trace and define sub-systems within the administrative system. They measure their interrelations, their interactions and how they affect each other. Such sub-systems include management sub-systems, personnel sub-systems, budget sub-systems and sub-systems for scheduling classes for students—lots of students. The result is a clear description of what things are like in the system and what is really accomplished. The third step calls for determining the objectives of the system and defining what it takes to achieve optimal performance. The result is a description of what ought to be accomplished. There may be more than one way to achieve optimal performance. Step four involves examining alternatives procedures, estimating their feasibility and acceptability and projecting their cost effectiveness. Often step four involves the design of a computer based model of the system to test, through simulation, the merits of alternative proposals. The result is a description of some alternative ways things might be done if the objectives are to be accomplished.

SDC stress the fact that these alternatives and their supporting evidence are then presented to the decision makers who have been involved in the exercise since it began, and it is their responsibility to arrive at decisions based on careful appraisal of the problem and its overall context. This is the goal of the system analysis: to make available to decision makers in government, municipal or state affairs, commerce or industry all the vital information so that they can make up their own minds as to the action to take.

The raw material of systems analysis is information gathered from a great many sources. This has to be examined, classified, organised, processed in whatever way is thought necessary and finally used. At the head of the system there is the information processing machine.

A great deal of mumbo jumbo has been written about systems analysis and it has built up its own strange jargon. It is, however, essentially a data gathering process followed by an evaluation as objective as possible of this data. It is often rendered extremely complicated because of the complications inherent in the environment and, in what might at first seem a relatively straightforward study, it is later found that experts in many different fields have to be consulted; an analysis may take months or even several years to complete. The objective is to provide the client with a design or formula for tackling a problem that offers a reasonable chance of success. For example, SDC has just begun an analysis of a new transportation system designed to cope with a particularly vexing problem that grows out of the megalopolitan traffic jam. The systems analysts, working jointly with personnel from the sponsoring agency, the Los Angeles City Department of Airports, is conducting analyses to establish preliminary system configurations and specifications, operational characteristics, construction and operating costs and is exploring the interactions between the 'Sky-Lounge' (name of new system) and local surface transportation systems. Furthermore, as part of the study, the team will establish criteria for determining helicopter sites, air and surface routes, fare structures, service schedules, facilities, maintenance and personnel requirements for the system. As a direct result of this work the client, the Los Angeles City Department of Airports, will be able to determine both the strengths and weaknesses of the system and have all the information available to them to help make it more efficient.

The success achieved by the new technology depends to a large degree upon the extent of the cooperation and collaboration obtained from the decision makers who, from the beginning of an analysis, have to be closely involved with the work.

Systems analysis is not a panacea; indeed it is much more applicable to problems where the technical content is predominant than to sociological problems. It does not provide decision makers with neat, straightforward solutions to their problems, but it does set out the guidelines enabling them the choice of alternative methods of tackling these problems with some reasonable chance of success.

Seminars

Hudson find seminars to be one of their best research tools because they force confrontation and illumination of the issues that underlie policy disagreements among the staff.

Seminars help to induce the staff to absorb each other's vocabulary and otherwise react with each other and to join issue on the assumptions, calculations and questions of fact that determine their differences. A great deal is also learned when expert and knowledgeable audiences are invited to seminars. Hudson stress the fact that seminars provide the means of subjecting ideas to systematic consideration, discussion and criticism, both by experts and by men of broad experience and judgement. In this way they gain inputs to both technical policy and public policy aspects of studies and also test their efforts to communicate in a useful way to senior decision makers.

Presentations at Hudson seminars are informal and non-technical, including enough detailed content to occupy the professional while remaining sufficiently straightforward and expository to challenge the non-professional. The underlying idea is to make explicit the relationships among such factors in policy problems as cultural tradition, economic development, military policy and international politics. The overall effect is to challenge existing world-views and to present alternatives. In addition to a programme of special seminars, Hudson present a number of special seminars and programmes for a particular occasion or in connection with individual contracts.

Problems Affecting the New Technologies' Effect on Society

The Harvard University Program on Technology and Society is a think tank that sets out to try and answer some of the urgent questions relating to the effect of the new technologies on society. It was founded in 1964 by a grant from the International Business Machines Corporation to undertake an enquiry in depth into the effects of technological change on the American economy, on public policies and on the character of society, as well as into the reciprocal effects of social progress on the nature, dimensions and directions of scientific and technological developments.

Many questions about how technology affects man, how it affects work and the constitution and structure of society, although vital to the future, remain unanswered and although an autonomous technology uncontrollable by man can be reserved for science fiction, there is little doubt that the more technologically oriented a society becomes the less able are man and nature to adapt themselves to the new conditions. Technology provides wonderful opportunities and new freedoms; it cures disease, increases the life span, gives us cheap and abundant energy, efficient communications and means of transportation, etc., but it also provides many problems. Technology is directly responsible for pollution of the environment and potential damage to the ecology of the planet, it causes social unrest, threatens the privacy and freedom of the individual and is directly responsible for a great deal of social and psychological malaise.

In the book *Perils of the Peaceful Atom* by Richard Curtis and Elizabeth Hogan, the authors draw attention to the deathly menace of nuclear garbage, predicting that if nuclear power grows as the experts predict, 6000 million curies of strontium 90 will have been accumulated in the United States alone, enough to kill 6000 million people and 30 times as much strontium 90 as would be released in a nuclear war. According to this book there are grave doubts about technology's ability to store nuclear waste indefinitely—and it remains violently lethal for more than 1000 years.

In the United States, the Government is becoming so worried about negative effects of technology that special machinery in the form of Technology Assessment Boards are likely to be set up to study the problems and to foresee potentially damaging effects of technology on nature and man. According to Dr Emmanuel Mesthene of Harvard University the attention of these boards is likely to be specially directed to the following:

1 Development of a system of social indicators to help gauge the social effects of technology.
2 Establishment of some body of social advisers to the President to help develop policies in anticipation of such effects.
3 Strengthen the role of the social sciences in policy making.

Think Groups

One of the interesting ways in which think tanks like Harvard University Program on Technology and Society is approaching problems relating to the interaction of technology and society is by Think Groups made up of scholars in a number of disciplines, business administration, economics, education, history, mathematics and engineering, philosophy, political science and sociology. Describing the work of the Think or Study Group, Dr Mesthene, a Director of the Program, says:

'There is almost no issue, document, idea or body of data of possible relevance to the Program's interest that does not come within the purview of the Study Group. A theme may be subjected to an informal preliminary exchange of ideas or to a more systematic effort at intellectual structuring. A pertinent recent article may be examined in detail for its illumination of some problematic issue or for new ideas it might contain. A scholar or decision maker anywhere who has knowledge or experience of any area of potential interest to the Program is invited to join the Group. . . .'

This probing by experts in different disciplines, something that never happens outside think tanks, is producing some interesting results. As Dr Mesthene, in referring to the work of these Think Groups points out: 'Even our less successful efforts this far, I believe, contribute to a gradual accumulation of intellectual capital that should yield significant dividends as we move further with our examination of fundamental questions.'

The work of organisations like the one at Harvard is designed primarily to help the wider research and policy making communities determine more precisely where lie the essential interrelations of technology and society and which seem most in need of added understanding. Think groups, if they achieve no other purpose, help to frame the right kind of questions and so prepare the way towards a more logical attempt to answer them. One valued ciriticism of the Think Group is that certain undesirable psychological factors are liable to play too big a part, what Dalkey and Helmar call 'specious persuasion, unwillingness to abandon publicly expressed opinions and the bandwagon effect of majority opinion.' However, Dr Mesthene does not seem to be too worried about this and stresses the fact that the members of the group are very carefully chosen and that there is a general willingness to work and to talk together without rancour. In his own words:

'The members of the group soon met the first requirement of success by sharing a mutual personal regard and intellectual respect that have made possible a genuinely free and objective exchange of ideas which precludes recourse either to personal sensitivities or to unilateral pretensions of professional privilege. It has been refreshing to observe a scholar generalise from the evidence of his special field only to be disputed by his colleague—often violently, but never with malice either intended or imputed—on the basis of equally pertinent but wholly other evidence from a different field. It has been satisfying to detect the wonder in both as each discovered the other's world, and exciting, above all, to glimpse the richer understandings and insights potential in the synthesis of the several perspectives.'

While the Delphi written questionnaire technique, generally applicable to forecasting, can also be used for problem solving in such fields as the effect of technology on society, the framing of the questions presents great difficulties, and the necessity for oversimplification of the answers is sometimes responsible for ill balanced judgements.

Scenarios

Another very useful tool used by the analyst in his study of a problem is the scenario. This attempts to provide a word picture of the background of the problem, describes in detail the environment, forecasts events and then consequences. A number of scenarios may have to be prepared, each one attempting to provide more data and a more critical appreciation of the position. A well written scenario can be of the greatest help in clarifying certain obscure situations and in providing the analyst with the kind of information he needs, in the form best suited to his 'report' requirements.

12 THINK TANKS AND INNOVATION

*Research pursues the unknown. By itself, research does not
really cost much. Applying the results of research, however, often
involves taking risks which are enormous. Is the degree of risk
always proportionate to the degree of innovation?*

ARTHUR D. LITTLE, INC.

Innovations and inventions are produced by man's endeavour
to meet clearly formulated needs dictated by new, challenging
and sometimes perilous situations, such as great national
programmes like defence and space in the USA and economic
empire building in Japan, threats of war and, in business,
intense competition. The success of Sputnik frightened the
Americans so badly that it caused them not only to revise and
revitalise their entire space programme, but to expand their
whole educational system even going to the extent of copying
the Russians by setting up schools for specially gifted children,
and to foster and to sponsor ambitious research programmes in
universities, industry and independent research centres, such
as think tanks. Although it is fashionable to condemn America's
$24 billion Apollo programme as sheer waste of money and the
point has been made that moon dust works out at $110 million
a kilogram, this is really cooking the books. The American
public has not, as the authors of *Journey to Tranquility* point out,
been the victims of a grand self-delusion. The man-in-space
programme has greatly accelerated the rate of innovation in a
number of vital industries, such as electronics, instruments,
computers, solid fuel, metallurgy, fibres, glass, plastics and
acted as a pace setter in many others. There may not be
diamonds on the moon but there is a vast business potential in
space satellites and space stations making possible greatly

improved communication and weather forecasting as well as opening up entirely new and rich fields of geological exploration. It has also encouraged the development of new and revolutionary management techniques, such as Programme Evaluation Review Techniques (PERT) and Critical Path Method (CPM), while the Planning—Programming–Budgeting System (PPBS) is another example of technology transfer that is today proving invaluable in non-military spheres.

Wars and the threat of war have always been a forcing house for innovations and inventions and man's most notable advances in technology have been made as a direct result of these pressures. The First World War provided the right kind of impetus to get aviation off the ground while the Second World War gave us radar, the rocket, the atom bomb and anti-biotics—a queer mixture.

Ideas, discoveries and inventions often lie dormant for many years before the right conditions are present or the incentives powerful enough to convert them from theory into practice. The classic example is, of course, radar, the principles of which were known to science since the early experiments of the German physicist Heinrich Hertz in 1887 who discovered that metallic objects can reflect radio waves. Although a great deal of experimental work was done on radio waves by the Americans, Taylor, Young, Hyland and others (pulse radar was actually discovered in 1930 by Hyland and Young) it was not until the threat of the Second World War that governments realised the great military potential of this device. In 1935 the Scottish physicist Watson-Watt persuaded the Committee for the Scientific Survey of Air Defence to try out the idea and so make radar available to help Britain win its crucial air battle, the Battle of Britain.

The atmosphere most favourable to innovation and invention in business is one where the entrepreneurial spirit is encouraged and where success is amply rewarded. One of the reasons given for Britain's poor return for its massive national investment in R & D is that it no longer encourages the entrepreneur and the current tax system does nothing to help. As many economists have pointed out, things are very different in the United States where the tax system is sufficiently flexible to allow for losses in the early years of development to be offset against any future profits.

The industrial spin off from our universities is disappointingly small. Neither Oxford nor Cambridge nor, indeed, any other

British university has anything even remotely approaching Route 128 around Boston, Massachusetts which draws off so much talent and inspiration from MIT or Palo Alto, California from Stanford University.

No one doubts that in Britain's research laboratories there lies a rich harvest of potentially valuable ideas awaiting development; the great pity is that not enough of them find outlets in industry. Moreover, Britain's concentration of R & D manpower in MinTech is too remote from the market place, too closely aligned with classified material to contribute very much to industry and the research associations (50 per cent financed by MinTech) are too poor and too parochial to do more than satisfy the immediate research requirements of the industries they serve. What is needed in Britain today is a few establishments like Battelle Memorial Institute and Stanford Institute where contract research on the American pattern can be carried out, and it would seem as if the Government is beginning to realise that there is something to be said for this arrangement. Indeed, it looks as if a publicly based contract research organisation may one day be set up, possibly by an extension of the work of the National Research Development Corporation (NRDC) which so far has only been responsible for the commercial development of fairly advanced projects.

How could a contract research organisation like Battelle or Stanford help in speeding up the rate of innovation in a particular company? First by studying its environment and its customers and trying to assess their needs; studying the state-of-the-art of technology applicable to the company in terms of the findings of non-mission and mission research, materials, techniques and trends; examining the size, shape and pattern of the competition and trying to gain some kind of picture of how it will emerge 10 and 15 years ahead. In effect, to try and determine tomorrow's needs and so provide a pattern for the guidance of research and development in their search for the most promising projects on which to deploy their forces. By applying some of the latest techniques of normative forecasting a great deal can be learned about future needs. Indeed, one definition of normative forecasting is 'goal or needs oriented planning' and the classic example is, of course, America's Apollo programme. Here the objective was clearly defined— to put a man on the moon in x number of years—probability of success or failure assessed, cost estimated (although it was wildly out), the various approaches to the goal examined and a step by step analysis made of them. In the sphere of business a similar kind of approach can be equally useful, except that here it is the function of market research to determine changing patterns of need and opportunity and to provide the guidelines for choosing objectives for possible R & D.

There is certainly no lack of potentially useful 'technological finds' but to be really useful these have to be need oriented, that is, related to a specific marketing outlet. Industry today suffers from too much information and stands in peril of being buried under a great pile of unread reports, summaries, surveys and the like. Communications have run amok. The great difficulty facing modern management is to find people who can distil from this mountain of information facts vital to a specific problem, not an easy task as it calls for a good technological background, imagination and business judgement and something of a flair for looking into the future.

Charles N. Kimball, President of Midwest Research Institute, points out that:

> 'The technical entrepreneur, the champion of a new idea, is frequently the main force behind technical change. His strength may be enthusiasm, ingenuity, and a commercial or public purpose and not a basic research point of view. He may be more distinguished for these attributes than for his lecturical expertise. His role is a vital constituent of transfer and innovation.'

It is know that some industries enjoy an exceptionally high rate of innovations, notably electronics, computers, instruments, plastics, aerospace, etc., and this, of course, creates an environment favourable to change, to innovation. Managements in these science based industries tend to be more receptive to new ideas than managements in other industries and as a result more encouragement is given to inventiveness and the imaginative approach. However, for these industries competition tends to be exceptionally keen, each firm watching its neighbour very carefully and there is a marked tendency for smaller companies to play safe by following in the wake of the leaders. It is only by a careful study of a company's environment that all the factors likely to influence the rate of innovations can become known.

The marketing structure can have a big influence not only on the ability of the company to generate new products but on the probability of success. Generally speaking a company satisfying several markets, for example a manufacturer supplying paints, wallpaper, adhesives, brushes and applicators, is in a better position to generate an entirely new product, such as vinyl floor tiles, than a firm catering for just one market, for instance a firm supplying only paint. Not only has the multi-market manufacturer a comprehensive range of outlets offering opportunities for the absorption of product innovations, but the mentality of his marketing organisation is usually better fitted to handle new products, particularly if they look like satisfying growth markets, than the more conservative manufacturer.

Think tanks, because of the marriage of business skills to scientific disciplines, have the necessary expertise to relate environmental conditions to product innovation policy more precisely than is usually possible within the company itself. Moreover the outside consultant is less likely to be affected by political or personal considerations. It could happen, for instance, that an entirely new product, such as vinyl floor tiles, might cause a major upheaval of the marketing organisation calling for the recruitment of new staff and the canvassing of a new type of customer, whereas the introduction of a complementary product, such as vinyl wallpaper, would make possible the better use of the sales staff and general promotional activities. No company is entirely self-sufficient and faced with a growing complexity of technologies, an overlapping of markets and greatly increased competition there is likely to be a greater need than ever for the business oriented think tank.

Modern technology and research are able to offer such a rich harvest of new ideas and innovations that very often the difficulty lies not so much in seeking but in finding—finding applications to match the discoveries which science is pouring out, as the backlog of ideas, theories and inventions from the past, some of which remain dormant for many years before they are developed. The alkali–cellulose reaction of John Mercer (1850) was accorded an incubation period of 40 years and at the end of that time rediscovered and rapidly developed as an industrial process that was to revolutionise the cotton side of the textile industry. 'Mercerised' cotton fabrics led directly to the discovery of artificial silk (viscose) by Cross and Bevan (1892). Even far removed from technological processes, the planner's modern multi-storey car park is not a particularly novel idea: Leonardo di Vinci designed multi-storey stables!

Think tanks are exceptionally well placed to help industry by making available 'technical intelligence'. For example, at the

9

Midwest Research Institute an important feature of their work involves the gathering and interpretation of scientific and economic information from a wide variety of sources and bringing the total result to bear upon a particular problem. At MRI the processing of technical intelligence and the interpretation of technology include:

1 Concept identification.
2 Technical evaluation.
3 Market appraisal.
4 State-of-the art reviews.
5 Prediction of trends.
6 Creativity and invention.
7 Projection of new applications.
8 Dissemination to users.

Midwest is carrying out a unique programme in the field of 'technical intelligence' for the National Aeronautics and Space Administration. This programme identifies development in the space programme which have likely industrial applications; evaluates those ideas in terms of the needs of industries at various levels; documents and acquires the necessary information in a form useful to such industries; disseminates the new knowledge to forms identified as most likely users. The industrial programme is being broadened to develop specialised information sources for specific industries or regions and the appropriate dissemination and transfer techniques.

Although managements may give lip service to innovation, there is often a big resistance to change, particularly radical changes in technology involving new sources of raw materials, modification of plant and processing techniques and perhaps a new approach to marketing with the prospect of dealing with different types of customers. This resistance to change is, of course, to be expected; any company that accepts it too readily is unstable. Indeed a large number of people view innovation with apprehension. In the early days of the Rand Project the Rand team met a good deal of opposition from the Air Force who feared that too drastic a change in programmed activity might well be interpreted as an 'admission of error on a large scale' and that this could undermine confidence and destroy morale. Wherever one looks there is always a resistance to change!

How to take the uncertainty out of product innovation has preoccupied management consultants for years and so far no one has yet come up with a sure recipe for success. R & D is by its very nature an uncertain business and no one can be quite sure that the desired goals will ever be attained, or that if they are attained they will be exactly the same as the planners had in mind originally. It is rare that a new product or process matches up to the expected specifications when it emerges from the laboratory. There has always to be a certain amount of re-thinking and re-shaping of policies and business strategies when it has settled down. When polyethylene was discovered, ICI was certain that because of its excellent electrical insulating properties it would find its biggest outlets in the electrical field. As it turned out, however, by far the biggest single market for polyethylene is in packaging as a film for wrapping. In this application, properties other than electrical insulation were exploited, such as transparency, moisture resistance, ease of heat sealing, etc.

Inventions to succeed need to appear at the right time, a time favourable to their development. Faraday's great success in linking electricity with magnetism making possible the practical introduction of a new source of power was only possible because society in his day was power conscious. The industrial revolution was thirsting for new sources of power. The social needs of the time dictate the kind of inventions that are likely to succeed. Today, with the growing emphasis on communications the times are highly favourable to innovations in this field. The perfection of machines to mass produce goods created the right conditions for the development of plastics, materials that are better suited than the traditional materials to conversion into goods by moulding and extrusion.

To be successful the new product or process has to fit into the general pattern of business and the state-of-the-art of the technology involved. The vision telephone has been on the shelf some years waiting for the very high capacity cables to be installed. However, even when these cables are laid it is not envisaged that the vision phone on its own will be an immediate commercial success, although alongside other new developments, such as Confravision, forecasters predict that eventually it may prove a profitable innovation. Contrary to what many people think, very few inventions are accidental like Röntgen's discovery of X-rays, but in the history of science it is not unusual to find one discovery sparking off another or at least leading to or prompting another field of research. Röntgen's X-rays led directly to Henri Becquerel's discovery of radio activity.

From the time of Roger Bacon (1214–94) discoveries and

inventions have been made, lost and made again. The magnetic knowledge of Peter Peregrinus in the thirteenth century recalled by Gilbert in the sixteenth; the isochronous property of the pendulum known in the fourteenth and fifteenth century by the Arabs was rediscovered by Galileo at the end of the sixteenth. The history of science is rich in similar examples.

Invention tends to be a continuing process and it is very seldom that one person has been solely responsible for an invention. This is brought out very clearly in a study carried out by the Illinois Institute of Technology Research Institute on 'Technology retrospect and critical events for science' in which an attempt is made 'to examine the role of research in the overall process which leads eventually to technological innovation'. Of the five major technological innovations examined approximately 70 per cent were non-mission research, 20 per cent mission oriented research and 10 per cent development and application. Looking at just one of these innovations, the electron microscope, IITRI found that at the beginning of the twentieth century the electron miscroscope, as a concept, did not exist in anyone's mind, although crude images had been formed using cathode rays many years before. As Brüche noted in 1957, the 25th anniversary of the instrument:

> 'However, we would like to point out that the step from the recognition of the electron lens to the concept of the electron microscope even today is not a trivial one because it demands a mental re-orientation which experience has shown is even difficult for a physicist. Nobody, it is quite clear, would have dared to think that by the use of electrons the resolution limits of the light microscope could be pushed further out by several orders of magnitude. When considering that a rather obvious conclusion had not been drawn at the time, one has to remember how absurd the conclusion would have appeared then. Indeed, the magnetic electron lens appeared first as a curiosity and did not stimulate further development of the search for the electrical analogy.'

In their search for growth products and growth markets companies often need outside help in recognising business opportunities when they exist and in planning the development work which needs to be carried out. The real impulse for product innovation comes from the market place and not the laboratory. Industry is rich in examples of where academic research has been made to yield new materials whenever the right conditions were known to exist for their exploitation. The most important new dyestuffs discovered during the last 20 years, 'Procion dyes', depended on the existence and knowledge of cyanuric chloride, the history of which goes back to the first quarter of the nineteenth century.

Another example is silicone resins. During the period 1899 to 1944 Professor Kipping of Nottingham University College carried out a lifetime research on the silicon/carbon compounds but this aroused little interest outside the confined academic field. It was not until a search began for new types of electrical insulating materials able to withstand high temperatures that men, and particularly one man, Dr J. F. Hyde of the Corning Glass Works in America, began to look closely at Kipping's sticky resinous compounds and to realise their great potential. The Dow Corning Corporation is now the largest manufacturers of silicones in the world, supplying these resins for hundreds of specialised applications.

Think tanks like A. D. Little Inc. are very close to the market place and have had great success in product planning, in thinking up the type of new products or modifications of existing products most likely to fill the gaps in existing markets and in making the whole process of product innovation systematic and reproducible instead of being awkward and untidy. What the think tanks are particularly well qualified to do is to help business men find answers to such questions as:

1 What part has basic research to play in product proliferation?
2 What area of professional speciality is most likely to help in developing new products?
3 What product types should be developed?
4 What are current needs?
5 How is it possible to survive without making too many changes?

Some success has been achieved in stimulating creativity by novel means, such as modifications of the old brainstorming idea. A. D. Little Inc. have long operated 'invention groups' made up of small groups of individuals carefully selected for their technical skills and inventiveness, who have contracted to invent a new product or a new use for an old one.

Sherman Kingsbury of A. D. Little describes the work of

'invention groups' in the book *Uncertainty in Research Management and New Product Development* published by his company.

> 'These groups have been strongly committed to the examination of their own processes of work. Their aim is to learn guidelines to their successful styles of work as well as to learn to recognise signals that the group is in flight and to formulate ways of judging what was the meaning of the flight.'

Little have been working with two basic invention groups:

1 'Family' groups of individuals who share responsibility for specific innovative work in a given area and join with some members of ADL staff experienced in technology and in group skills.
2 'Heterogeneous' groups, in which people of diverse and appropriate skills join in a group setting to seek innovative concepts in a particular product area, even though this area is not in each member's regular area of corporate responsibility and normal placement in the organisation.

The groups meet for one and a half to three days at roughly monthly intervals with two to four consultants and usually the meetings are held outside the office in a hotel room. So far there does not appear to be any convincing evidence that 'invention groups' have achieved any outstanding success in creating new products but where they have been useful is in suggesting changes in the organisation's framework, product planning and in evolving new business strategies.

BIBLIOGRAPHY

LINDBLOM, CHARLES E., *The Policy Making Process* (Free Press, New York).

DANKOF, CLARENCE H., *Government Contracting and Technological Change* (Brookings Institution, Washington D.C.).

NELSON, RICHARD R., PECK, MERTON J. and KALACHEK, EDWARD D., *Technology, Economic Growth and Public Policy* (Brookings Institution).

SMITH, BRUCE L. R., *The Rand Corporation* (Harvard University Press, Massachusetts).

PRICE, DON K., *The Scientific Estate* (Harvard University Press, Massachusetts).

PRICE, DON K., *Government and Science* (New York University Press, New York).

CROZIER, MICHEL, *The Bureaucratic Phenomenon* (The University of Chicago Press, Chicago).

WALL STREET JOURNAL STAFF, *Here Comes Tomorrow! Living and Working in the Year 2000* (Don Jones Book, Princeton, USA).

BJERRUM, C. A., *Forecasts 1968–2000 of Computer Developments and Applications* (Parsons and Williams, Copenhagen).

RAMO, SIMON, *Cure for Chaos* (David McKay, New York).

ARGENTI, JOHN, *Corporate Planning: A Practical Guide* (Allen and Unwin, London).

WHYBARK, D. CLAY, *Forecasting Pilot and Mechanic Requirements and Pilot Supply for Civil Aviation* (Purdue University, Lafayette, Indiana).

PARSONS, S. A. J., *The Framework of Technical Innovation* (Macmillan, London).

GALTUNG, JOHAN, *Theory and Methods of Social Research* (George Allen and Unwin, London).

BUCHAN, ALISTAIR (Editor), *Europe's Futures, Europe's Choices* (Chatto and Windus, London).

MCHALE, JOHN, *The Future of The Future* (George Braziller, New York).

WHITE, S. J., *Dynamic Programming* (Oliver and Boyd, Edinburgh).

CALDER, NIGEL, *Technopolis* (MacGibbon and Kee, London).

MCQUAIL, DENNIS, *Towards a Sociology of Mass Communications* (Collier-Macmillan, London).

DENNING, BASIL, *Corporate Long Range Planning* (Longmans, London).

CETRON, MARVIN J., *Technological Forecasting: A Practical Approach.*

WILLS, GORDON, TAYLOR, B. and ASHTON, D. J. L., *Technological Forecasting and Corporate Strategy* (Crosby Lockwood).

EWALD, WILLIAM R. JNR. (Editor), *Environment Change and Environment and Policy* (Indiana University Press).

BRIGHT, JAMES R. (Editor), *Technological Forecasting for Industry and Government* (Prentice Hall International, Hemel Hempstead).

MICHAEL, DONALD N., *The Unprepared Society: Planning for a Precision Future* (Basic Book Inc., New York and London).

PARKHILL, D. F., *The Challenge of the Computer* (Addison–Wesley, Reading, Mass.).

GORDON, J. J. and HELMER, OLAF, *Report on a Long Range Forecasting Study* (The Rand Corporation Paper, P.2982, September 1964).

GORDON, J. J. and AMENT, H. R., *Forecasts of Some Technological and Scientific Developments and their Social Consequences* (IFF Report R.6, September 1969).

SCHREIBER, SERVAN J. J., *The American Challenge* (New York, Athenium).

KAHN, HERMAN and WIENER, ANTHONY J., *The Year 2000: A Framework for Speculation on the Next 30 Years* (Macmillan, New York).

GALBRAITH, J. K., *The New Industrial State* (Houghton Mifflin, Boston).

KOESTLER, ARTHUR, *The Yogi and the Commissar* (Cape, London).

FORRESTER, JAY W., *Urban Dynamics* (The MIT Press, Cambridge).

PECCEI, AURELIO, *The Chasm Ahead* (Macmillan, London).

HALL, ARTHUR D., *A Methodology for Systems Engineering* (Van Nostrand, Princeton).

WOLD, H. and JUREEN, L., *Demand Analysis* (John Wiley & Son, New York).

JANTSCH, ERICH, *Technological Forecasting in Perspective* (OECD, Paris).

CHASE, STUART, *The Most Probable World* (Harper and Row, New York).

MATSON, FLOYD W., *The Broken Image: Man, Science and Society* (Doubleday, New York).

NOVIDE, SHELDON, *The Careless Atom* (Houghton Mifflin, Boston).

ELLUL, JACQUES, *The Technological Society* (Alfred A. Knopf, New York).

The Delphi Method III: Use of Self-ratings to improve Group Estimate (The Rand Corporation RM-6115-PR. 1969).

DROI, YEHEZKEL, *Public Policymaking Re-examined* (Chandler Publishing Company, San Francisco).

HORROBIN, DAVID, *Science is Good* (MTP, Aylesbury, Bucks).

BRAY, JEREMY, *Decision for Government* (Victor Gollancz, London).

INDEX